D1219669

FAILING GRADES

A Teacher's Report Card
on Education in America

Also by Philip Bigler

IN HONORED GLORY: Arlington National Cemetery, The Final Post

WASHINGTON IN FOCUS: The Photo History of the Nation's Capital

FAILING GRADES
A Teacher's Report
Card On Education
in America

by Philip Bigler and Karen Lockard

VANDAMERE PRESS
a division of AB Associates

Published by
Vandamere Press
A Division of AB Associates
P.O. Box 5243
Arlington, Virginia 22205
USA

Copyright 1992 Vandamere Press. Cullum cartoon on page 17, copyright
Copley News Service, 1991; MacNelley cartoon on page 26, copyright
Tribune Media Services, 1991; Doonesbury cartoon on page 48, copyright
Universal Press Syndicate, 1991; Peanuts cartoon on page 66, copyright
UFS, Inc.; Doonesbury cartoon on page 138, copyright Universal Press
Syndicate, 1988.

ISBN 0-918339-19-7

Library of Congress Cataloging-in-Publication Data

Bigler, Philip.
    Failing grades : a teachers report card on education in America /
by Philip Bigler and Karen Lockard.
      p.   cm.
    Includes bibliographical refrences and index.
    ISBN 0-918339-19-7 : $16.95
    1. Education—United States. 2. Teachers—United States.
I. Lockard, Karen. II. Title.
LA217.2.B54 1992
370'.973—dc20   91-26714
                                          CIP

Manufactured in the United States of America. This book is set in New
Century Schoolbook by Scott Photographics of Riverdale, Maryland.

All rights reserved, which includes the right to reproduce this book or any
portion thereof in any form whatsoever, except as provided by U.S.
Copyright Law. For information contact Vandamere Press.

Dedication

To our students at Bethesda-Chevy Chase
and McLean High Schools.

Acknowledgements

Throughout the writing of *Failing Grades*, we have found many people anxious to share with us their experiences, to offer advice, and to provide expertise. To all of those special principals, teachers, parents, and students, we are grateful.

We would especially like to express our thanks to former Secretary of Education, William Bennett, who was kind enough to grant us a personal interview. At that time, we had the opportunity to discuss with him at length the current lamentable state of American education. His insights and comments proved not only informative but inspirational as well. Secretary Bennett's administrative assistant, Noreen Burns, was similarly kind and we would like to thank her for all of her time and help.

In many ways, the principal is the key to a successful school. Henry Gradillas and Ruby McClendon represent two of the nation's best and they provided us with a solid role model of educational leadership, administrative skill, and substantive reform—all of which are desperately needed in public schools today. Likewise, Elizabeth Lodal at McLean High School, thoughtfully reviewed our recommendations and helped refine them to ensure that they were practical and realistic. At Bethesda-Chevy Chase High School, Gladys McClain generously shared her expertise and wisdom. During the years we worked with her, she served as a strong, fair-minded administrator who selflessly dedicated herself to both students and teachers.

Penn State University football coach, Joe Paterno, is an outspoken advocate of the importance of academics in the lives of athletes. Paterno is a true educator and we are grateful for the work he does in helping show high school and college students that academics come first and foremost during their years in school. His message is ours as well. His wife, Sue, continues to inspire many young people by working as an athletic tutor and serving on the board of directors for the Special Olympics. Her personal warmth and professional concern for our project encouraged us as did her honesty about important issues. Authors Philip Hoose and Richard Lapchick also contributed greatly to our chapter on high school sports. At the National Endowment for the Humanities, Chairman Lynne Cheney provided expertise on the role of special interests in education and their part in contributing to the degeneration of quality in both textbooks and curricula.

Throughout the country, literally dozens of teachers contributed to this book. We were constantly impressed by their dedication, commitment, and professionalism. Some, though, for practical reasons, have requested to remain anonymous and we will respect and honor this right. At the same time, we would like to publicly express our thanks to them and to the following educators: Bob Appleton; Marlowe Adkins; Jessie Bachike; Ron Bombick; Diane Breakiron; Hope Burwell; Carolina Butler; Mike Carroll; Anna Citrino; Arlene Cohen; Cathy Colglazier; Ann Drew; Jeff Dunson; Bob Eikel; Carleen Fritz; Craig Gruber; Jay Headman; Evanthia Lambrakopoulos; Jeannie Lowrie; Bob Nakamura; Don Nall; Les Olinger; Lynn Owen; Rennie Pincus; Nancy Powell; Bob Sheridan; Lisa Startzman; Edie Tattel; Jon Virden; and Beth Weitz.

Although the schools have produced far too many students who are under-educated and ill-prepared for the modern world, there are many notable exceptions. In the course of writing *Failing Grades*, we have been privileged to be associated with some of the best students in the nation. Our gratitude goes especially to: Jonathan Adelman; Shelby Aikens; Jenny Bastress; Alex Eastman; Caroline Frick; Diane Kelleher; and Bryan Tanis. At the same time, we would like to express our appreciation to all of the students at both Bethesda-Chevy Chase and McLean high schools. Throughout this project, they have been a constant source of enthusiasm and encouragement.

In addition, we would like to thank the following parents and other educational professionals for their assistance: Nancy Adelman; Linda Aikens; Diane Jones; and Joe Standa. Others generously offered their time to help compile the index and to proofread the final manuscript: Cathy Colglazier, Kathy Kirk, Tom Mulhearn, and Wende Walsh. Candy Miller and Nadine Pryke deserve special thanks as well, for their last minute administrative assistance.

Any extensive project requires much time which Karen's husband, David, selflessly provided so that she could pursue this important undertaking. His love and understand were invaluable. Likewise, her children, Adam and Kate, cheered us both on and served as a very personal reminder why we were writing this book. Karen's parent's, Bob and Leah Oberheim, constantly offered their encouragement and love as did her mother and father-in-law, Claudia and Alan Lockard. Special thanks to her mother, Leah, for her very special guidance with this project. Advice from writers, Steve Lockard and Sonny Young was greatly appreciated along with the confidence shown by Suzanne Young. Karen would also like to offer special thanks to her dear friend, Kathy Kirk, an outstanding teacher who read, advised, coached, and enthusiastically backed us from the beginning. Phil's wife, Linda, has similarly shown patience in this and all of his other writing projects. Over the past six years, she has stoically endured shortened vacations, missed engagements, and countless other sacrifices to help Phil meet his many publication deadlines. Throughout this project, Phil's father, Charlie, was always available to help solve computer and software problems and to offer needed encouragement. Our love and thanks goes to them.

All of these people represent part of the growing coalition determined to reform American education. They give us reason for renewed hope and optimism concerning the future of our nation's public schools.

Table of Contents

An Introduction to
Education 101

"Youth is the best season wherein to acquire knowledge, tis a season when we are freest from care, the mind is then unincumbered & more capable of receiving impressions than in an advanced age—in youth the mind is like a tender twig, which you may bend as you please, but in age like a sturdy oak and hard to move."

ABIGAIL ADAMS

AMERICAN EDUCATION IS FAILING. As a nation, we are at imminent risk of losing an entire generation to a life of ignorance and illiteracy because public schools are not doing an acceptable job of preparing our young people for college, for careers, or for life in general. In *A Nation at Risk,* the National Committee on Excellence in Education concluded, "If an unfriendly foreign power had attempted to impose on America the mediocre educational performance that exists today, we might well have viewed it as an act of war. As it stands, we have allowed this to happen to ourselves . . . we have, in effect, been committing an act of unthinking, unilateral educational disarmament."

Countless statistics, studies, and reports support such dismal assessments. In the United States today, an estimated 23 million people are considered to be functionally illiterate while

26 percent of all 17-year-olds fail to graduate from high school. Yet despite these abysmal trends, spending of taxpayer dollars on education is at an all-time high. In 1991 alone, 384 billion dollars were allotted to education with the *average* per pupil expenditure soaring to over $5,500 per year despite decreased tax revenues and a major recession. The American public has a right, indeed a duty, to demand a realistic assessment of the current problems faced by public schools and to require teachers, administrators, parents, and politicians to implement positive, realistic measures for reform.

Historically, the purpose and mission of the American public schools was clearly defined and widely accepted. Teachers were expected to competently instruct all students in the basic disciplines—reading, writing, and arithmetic—as well as provide them with a solid base of history and an appreciation of American democracy. Few people questioned either the teacher's authority or the school's curriculum. By 1900, the country was transformed from a provincial nation of illiterates into an industrial society of proficient readers.

Teachers were leading the movement for educational reform. As a group, they advocated the implementation of new teaching techniques to humanize instruction; demanded that state governments impose compulsory education requirements to end the very real abuses of child labor; and called for extending the benefits of the educational system to newly arrived immigrants, minorities, and the economically deprived. Because of such noble efforts, teachers as a group were universally respected for their idealism and expertise.

As the nation became more suburban, school boards slowly abandoned the concept of the neighborhood school. School buses and improved highways made large, centralized high schools both practical and economical since students could be offered a greater variety of courses and more efficient services. Simultaneously, classroom teachers saw their influence on educational policy gradually eroded as an ever-expanding centralized school bureaucracy was created to support the public schools. Between 1960 and 1984, curriculum specialists and instructional supervisors increased by a staggering 500 percent while the overall number of classroom instructors grew by only 57 percent, leading to the modern system where 22 percent of all education professionals operate outside of the classroom, isolated from students and teachers alike. Principals, assistant principals, area superintendents, action teams, and curriculum specialists have come to dominate educational policy and monopolize upper level salary scales. In the American educational hierarchy, those furthest from the classroom and with the least direct contact with students have the most influence in establishing the curricula, focus, and agenda of the schools. The talented teacher who wishes to achieve professional advancement, gain recognition, and earn higher salary compensation, has virtually no alternative but to leave the classroom for administration. The upper regions of the educational bureaucracy are already top heavy. The National Endowment for the Humanities recognized the insanity of such a system maintaining, "Resources are increasingly being drawn into salaries for people who are not in the classroom but who attempt to direct the activity going on there. Specialists in education for the most part, they inevitably steer in the direction of process rather than content, toward skills rather than substance. How much better to spend this money giving teachers time and resources so they can work out teaching methods and gain greater command of the subjects they teach. How much better to put teachers, rather than outsiders, in charge of the classroom."

As a group, teachers have little say in educational reform and in such important matters as a school system's budget priorities, colleague evaluations, and staff hiring. They have even lost much of their autonomy in the classroom, as they are routinely required to execute unrealistic programs which are formulated in the inner recesses of the educational bureaucracy by so-called experts who are completely immune to the consequences of such measures. These policies and edu-

cational fads are predictably criticized for failing to address
the daily realities of the classroom environment or to meet
even the minimal needs of individual students. They are, instead, often fabricated for political purposes to generate impressive statistics for public relations campaigns and to create
the illusion of progress. Dr. Robert Appleton, a high school
history teacher for 27 years, argued, "[there is] a lack of connection between the school teacher and the administrator . . .
there is a tension between people who are educators—teachers—and those who run the schools. Teachers are really not
asked what the solutions are to the problems with education. . . . I trust teachers and I'm not sure that the system
does. Teachers are not being informed or told what is going
on; things are being managed by somebody else who is pretty
far away from the classroom."

Good principals can do much to lessen the adverse consequences of the massive educational bureaucracy. As the
school's on-site manager, they have enormous influence in
shaping the school's academic philosophy, improving staff morale, and enhancing student learning. Indeed, no single individual has a greater impact on the day-to-day operations of
the public schools. Despite this fact, far too many principals
in today's schools abrogate their leadership responsibilities
and do little to inspire good teaching or quality education.

The high school diploma, once the embodiment of a minimal
standard of achievement and a testament to a person's basic
functional abilities, now represents little more than a report
of adequate attendance. Colleges and universities complain
bitterly that professors are now forced to add remedial courses
to teach incoming freshman how to write simple sentences
and to compute basic mathematical formulas. Thirty-one percent of all incoming college freshmen currently enroll in such
basic courses, illustrating an obvious decline in standards.

American businesses have likewise been affected adversely
by the failure of schools to produce individuals capable of entering the professional world. Thomas Mulhearn, a corporate

personnel recruiter, observed, "I don't think that high school students are well prepared at all. [Businesses] want an employee to be able to read, do basic mathematics, and to be able to interact with other people. . . . Computers and automation are eliminating tremendous numbers of jobs and restructuring tremendous numbers of others. There are a lot of service oriented jobs but they are being reduced to the most menial, basic tasks you can find. . . . Those kinds of jobs are not going to be attractive. You can always find jobs sweeping floors; retail stores will always be looking for minimum wage sales clerks. But good, rewarding, satisfying jobs are disappearing for high school graduates and high school is the end for most people."

The relatively recent intrusion of politics into the classroom has clouded the true mission of education with a long list of conflicting social agendas. The public schools are no longer expected to just teach history, English, mathematics, and science, but instead must debate the merits of prayer in schools and the inclusion of the latest birth control methods in health courses. Virtually every social ill or problem that temporarily commands the nation's attention, is inevitably reduced to a matter that can be solved simply by "more education." Classroom teachers find themselves bewildered and frustrated, groping for answers to such complex issues as drug abuse, AIDS, racism, teen pregnancy, and a myriad of other social problems. These issues are constantly dumped on the schools where they languish between elections until they are once again resurrected by calculating politicians for yet another campaign. Robert Eickel, a former assistant principal believes that state legislatures ". . . create a good part of the problem, as well-intentioned as they might be . . . many of them know little or nothing about education or what's required to teach kids." He continued, "They are always mandating new kinds of things and then saying [to the schools], 'We pass the law and now you do it.' How are you supposed to accomplish these things?" Dr. Frederick Sample, Superintendent of the Bellefonte (Pa.) Area Schools, in an article in *State College Magazine,* agreed with such an assessment. He said, "I've begun to think perhaps we're putting too much into our schools. If we cut down on some things, we might be able to do an even better job. . . . Let's face it. We teach our students everything from driver's ed to calculus. It's too much."

American public schools have become social service agencies responsible for administering a wide variety of programs such as child care, free lunch programs, and basic parenting needs. Dr. Appleton observed, "I wish in education we could list the things that we could do competently and say the other things that we cannot do. . . . The school systems of the United States are under the added burden now of dealing with problems that were not considered to be a part of the school. The school now is a social service institution—free lunch programs, counseling service, making special arrangements for students. We have, for good or ill, taken on added responsibility."

The tragic and ongoing decline of the traditional American family has directly and adversely contributed to the ever increasing burden on American public schools. One teacher remarked, "There is a breakdown of the family as a cohesive unit that will deal with problems and issues. The public schools are predicated upon the idea that there is stability in the home and that there is someone there to bother and fuss over homework and getting your lessons done. Today's kids are not going home to that." Single-parent households are often the norm rather than the exception while two-parent families frequently find both spouses working outside the home. Still, parents are the single most important factor in a child's academic development, since even the most talented and inspirational secondary school teacher spends little more than five hours per week with a given student. Chester Finn, a former Assistant Secretary of Education, estimates that from birth to age 19, only 9 percent of a child's life is spent in school. The remaining time is the direct responsibility of the parent and it is precisely this out-of-school period that is most

Copyright 1991. CULLUM. Reprinted with permission of Copley News Service. All rights reserved.

crucial to a child's educational development. Yet far too many parents abdicate this crucial obligation in what amounts to middle class child abuse.

More young people are being left home alone, unsupervised and free to fill the days with whatever activities please them. Illicit drugs and narcotics are easily available to high school students and teen alcohol abuse has reached epidemic levels. A sense of youthful invulnerability has lead to unprecedented promiscuity, with 74 percent of high school seniors saying they have engaged in sexual intercourse despite ominous warnings of AIDS and venereal disease.

On a daily basis, television viewing continues to be one of the most persistent adversaries that face teachers. One survey showed that 64 percent of all 13-year olds (8th graders) watched over three hours of television per night, while in high school 40 percent of their 11th grade counterparts did the same, while boasting that they spent less than one hour per night on their homework. Although the recent introduction of cable television has increased both the variety and quality of educational programming, most young people opt for the lighter fare of the music video stations and the entertainment channels. Ted Koppel, the host of *Nightline,* lectured on the educational impact of television during a commencement address at Duke University: "We have learned, for example, that your attention span is brief. We should know; we helped make it that way. Watch 'Miami Vice' some Friday night. You will find that no scene lasts more than 10 to 15 seconds. Look at 'MTV' or 'Good Morning America' and watch the images and ideas flash past in a blur of impressionistic appetizers. No, there is not much room on TV for complexity. You can partake of our daily banquet without drawing on any intellectual resources, without either physical or moral discipline. We require nothing of you, only that you watch." Unfortunately, students take these bad habits into the classroom. Compared to the stimulation of a television docu-drama or the excitement of a rock video, it is little wonder that the hard academics of mathematics, the intellectual challenges of a science experiment, or the quiet eloquence of literature fail to capture their imaginations. Former vice principal Bob Eickel claimed, "Learning can be exciting. It can be fun." However, students have lost sight of the work ethic as part of the process of education. Eickel said, "Basically we are there to educate and not entertain. So much learning is pure and simple hard work." The premise that education is a two-way process that requires both teaching and learning is one that many educators feel has gone by the wayside in the classroom today and SAT scores continue to plummet.

Activists and zealots have targeted the public schools in a cynical effort to restructure courses and curricula to reflect their own personal political philosophies and values to the exclusion of other viewpoints. Some have made ludicrous efforts to ban literary classics while others have attacked the teaching of established scientific theories or denounced the efforts of educators to impose basic, minimal standards of behavior. The role of the special interest groups in education has led to the degeneration of textbooks and other classroom materials as publishers futilely attempt to produce course materials that will offend no one.

No group has been more betrayed by the American educational establishment than the nation's minorities. One local chapter of the NAACP accurately assessed the efforts of educating black youth as "a total and consistent failure." Over 55 percent of all minority students fail even to graduate from high school, by definition a minimal education in today's complex and demanding society. Reading levels for blacks and Hispanics rank far below the statistical norm as do mathematics skills. Many teachers complicate the problem by reducing their academic expectations for minority students thereby helping to perpetuate a continuing cycle of failure. For too many minorities, "the school" has become a foreboding and uncaring place which inevitably leads to days filled with alienation and frustration. By the year 2000, one-third of the students in the public schools will be from minorities, disadvantaged, or low-income groups.

School boards and administrators continually profess to be aware of this lamentable situation. Each new school year begins with widely publicized new programs allegedly designed to improve the achievement of minorities. Each year the programs fail because they lack innovation, understanding, and insight. The situation is intolerable. No civilized society can dismiss such a large portion of its population. There is no greater challenge facing American education today than improving the achievement of its growing minority populations.

America's competitiveness and leadership in the global economy of the 1990's is being seriously challenged. Many attribute this decline to the poor quality of education being offered to American students when compared to the high pressure, goal-oriented schools of the Germans and Japanese. Futurist Alvin Toffler in his newly published book, *The Power Shift,* argues that "our massive education systems are highly obsolete" and that to reassert America's leadership in the world "depend[s] on revolutionizing the education system . . . education is no longer merely a priority for parents, teachers, and a handful of educational reformers, but for [all society]." Despite such ominous warnings, far too many in the educational establishment resist change that might jeopardize their power. They are content with mediocrity and completely unwilling to reassess educational priorities and anachronistic practices.

America's schools need not fail as they move into the 1990's. The classroom is the basis of education and change is possible to enable schools to educate well. Vital factors that interfere with the education of today's youth are not common knowledge to most Americans. Even parents of school-age children fail to realize the complex components that influence teaching in the schools that their children attend. It is necessary to look closely at the diverse elements that are contributing to the evolution of the public school into something very different from the schools attended by any American over the age of 30.

Examination and evaluation of existing ills can lead to the reformation of public schools into institutions that excel at serving the needs of all American children. American schools currently are succeeding with some students, yet failing to reach an increasingly large group of others. Analyzing current school problems clarifies why education is failing so many. The critical issue of change may then be addressed, so that America's public schools will not be doomed to failing grades.

The Principal

Power

"We have entered an age in which education is not just a luxury
... [but] a necessity without which a person is defenseless in
this complex, industrialized society."

LYNDON B. JOHNSON

THE TRADITIONAL NEIGHBORHOOD SCHOOL of the past has vanished. No longer are important, fundamental, educational issues entrusted to teachers, principals, and parents, but are consigned instead to a large, impersonal, centralized bureaucracy of invisible administrators who dictate policy rather than allow reason and expedience to govern education. The superintendent of schools is at the head of this new educational hierarchy. Often generously blessed with a six-figure salary, most superintendents view the public schools as their personal domain to be ruled and manipulated with a monarch's disdain for democracy and disagreement.

Each year, superintendents are expected to establish their school system's educational priorities by preparing its annual operating budget. Aided by a large staff of accountants, assistants, secretaries, and bureau chiefs, the superintendents wield enormous power that allows them to autocratically impose a vast array of new programs and pet projects designed to define and punctuate their tenure, all of which are liberally funded at the expense of teacher salaries, needed textbook acquisitions, important field trips, and other school-based activities. Little wonder that in most school systems, classroom teachers perceive their superintendents as adversaries rather than as allies, especially as their salaries and benefits are cut during a recession.

Beneath the superintendent is a vast array of so-called support services ranging from curriculum specialists to procurement agents to personnel officers. All are ostensibly hired to help teachers and the schools by expediting needed services. In reality, these staff members are often former teachers who have willingly abandoned the classroom for higher salaries and a life free from the hassles of teaching. They continually justify their existence by generating massive amounts of paper work, red tape, and new rules that continually frustrate efficiency and serve only to anger the competent educational professional. According to the editors of the *Washington Monthly,* this new breed of educational bureaucrats "spend their days churning out complicated memos that say nothing . . . place unnecessary and irrelevant burdens on teachers without helping them do their jobs, [and] are doing their part to doom American children." Indeed, major repairs take weeks to accomplish, equipment requisitions are ignored, and legitimate teacher requests languish in offices which never operate with a sense of urgency or dispatch. One teacher recounted in frustration that it took two written requests and three weeks for his desk drawer to be repaired. The county's centralized maintenance office detailed three people for a job that required two nails and less than two minutes of time. In such an inane system, good teachers and principals quickly learn that they must avoid bureaucratic mandates in order to remain effective and efficient.

The public school administrator closest to the classroom, with the most direct contact with teachers, is the principal. Certainly no single individual is more important to the school setting or to its daily operation than the principal who maintains a safe, orderly environment that is conducive to learning. A skilled, caring, hard working administrator can literally transform a school into an exciting learning environment with good teacher morale and eager students. Conversely, the arbitrary, dictatorial principal can quickly sour even the best of schools and build an impenetrable wall of resentment and alienation.

No job in the educational hierarchy is more consistently difficult nor carries with it more responsibility. According to Lynn Owen, the assistant principal of Magnolia Middle School in suburban Baltimore, principals are entrusted with the care and maintenance of a multi-million dollar building; they must manage a complex budget consisting of hundreds of transactions with expenditures worth thousands of dollars; and they must supervise and work with dozens of diverse teachers along with being directly responsible for the lives of children and the welfare of staff.

Ideally, the principal is the school's most conspicuous educational leader. The best principals actively support teachers by protecting the school day for learning and keeping classroom interruptions to a minimum. In essence, they ensure that quality instruction is going on in the classroom.

Yet despite a general consensus concerning the importance of maintaining a serious academic climate, many high schools throughout the United States experience an endless stream of interruptions, assemblies, PA announcements, and other disruptions of instruction, making it difficult for even the most talented teachers to effectively plan or complete required curriculum objectives. In one suburban high school, the faculty openly complained that October had been unofficially designated by the administration as "National No-teach" month. During that month alone, the school's schedule was seriously modified for three school-wide assemblies, a 1/2 day teacher in-service, and state-wide functional reading and math tests. Classes were also disrupted by four fire alarms (only one

Copyright 1991. Jeff MacNelly. Reprinted by permission: Tribune Media Services.

scheduled), the painting of rooms and hallways, and a county mandate that no homework or assignments be given in any subjects during the Jewish holiday of Sukhot. Likewise various students missed classes or were dismissed early for college visits, six field trips, a band performance at an elementary school, and for over 30 "extracurricular" athletic events ranging from field hockey to tennis. When taken in conjunction with routine absences for illness, doctor appointments, meetings with guidance counselors, and suspensions, the subtle but unmistakable message the school conveyed to its entire student body was that classroom activities were not important and could be interrupted at will.

Principals must also be skilled managers of their faculty and staff, aware of individual strengths and weaknesses. Classes should be assigned according to talent, and individual exemplary performance should be regularly acknowledged. Most principals, however, extend professional recognition and respect only to the high profile, charismatic teachers or to the openly self-promoting. Athletic coaches continually garner praise through mandatory attendance pep rallies and in a seemingly endless stream of announcements featuring stories of game-day heroics. Far too many principals simply reduce a successful school year to a winning football or basketball season. Don Nall, a middle school teacher in Kentucky, recalled how his principal clearly gave priority to the school's sports program by generously providing one of the school's football coaches several days of paid administrative leave to attend a coaching clinic and covered all of his expenses. When Nall made a similar request for academic leave, it was flatly denied. Nall said, "I was invited by then Vice President Mondale to present a paper [in Washington, D.C.] to a White House Conference on Education . . . I went and was docked three day's pay . . . I question still the priorities."

Since many principals fail to treat their staff as competent professionals, classroom teachers must derive their career satisfaction exclusively from their daily interaction with students. Despite the hardships and routine crises confronted in the classroom, it is these important relationships that educators cherish most and from which they draw virtually their entire professional satisfaction. Rarely do they receive a word of encouragement or even a simple thank you for their efforts.

In many high schools, principals are merely another faceless bureaucrat, known only by a few favored or infamous students. They seldom interact with teachers, and seem content in the splendid isolation and seclusion of their offices. To both staff and students, such individuals are little more than an eerie voice that sometimes interrupts classes over the school's public address system or a mysterious figure that makes an occasional appearance at a sporting event or assembly.

Truly outstanding principals are an exception in American education with only 15 percent rated excellent by their faculties. The best, though, are a recognizable force within the school building. One such exemplary principal explained, "A principal who is doing his job should have a lot of contact with kids. He should be the one visiting the classrooms . . . [and] should be a presence in the school."

While many principals relish the opportunity to leave the building to attend area-wide meetings and formal luncheons, Dr. Henry Gradillas, the former principal of Garfield High School in the city of Los Angeles and an inspirational educational reformer, strongly maintains that a successful principal must assume responsibility for what is happening in the school. Area administrative meetings held off campus during the school day posed a major problem. Gradillas recalled, "I told them, 'If I leave the school, someone has to be placed in charge. No—this is where I belong. Read it to me, send it to me by mail, call your meetings on Saturdays, call it on Sunday, call it at night.' [But] no, they called them right in the middle of prime time . . . [when] the principal must be there in the rooms watching the delivery of instruction."

Some enlightened principals even continue to teach a class in addition to their administrative duties in order to keep current with educational methodology and to have more direct contact with students. Elizabeth Lodal, the principal of Mc-Lean High School in Fairfax County, Virginia, currently teaches a course entitled "Facing History and Ourselves." When asked why she returned to the classroom, Lodal explained, "Teaching is at the heart of why I do this job. I went into this business to teach and the biggest drawback to being a principal is that it takes you away from the classroom." Still, it required a strong commitment to balance her daily administrative duties with that of an instructor. Lodal, however, realized that "it sends a message to the faculty that the principal is committed to the educational process." To further increase her interaction with students, Mrs. Lodal also volunteers each year to substitute one day for every English teacher in the school. This not only frees the teachers to attend workshops and seminars, it guarantees that the principal has some direct contact with each and every student in the school.

Teachers universally agree that one characteristic of good principals is that they support their teachers, especially in matters of discipline. A lack of consistency and firmness can destroy a faculty's credibility. Throughout the course of any school year, teachers are confronted with literally hundreds of situations that require their professional judgement, based upon both training and experience, and they must have confidence that they will not be overruled for trivial reasons by a callous administrator.

One popular history teacher remembered that during a lesson, he had carefully divided his class into several small groups. Each had been assigned a special project to complete and to formally present. "John Wilson" was a problem student in the class, a young man who hated the world, despised school, and who posed daily discipline problems. For the most part, the teacher had been able to effectively deal with John's behavior although John remained a constant source of frustration and it had been virtually impossible to teach the boy any history. During this current assignment, John unleashed a stream of graphic curses towards his group leader, a shy young girl who had only insisted that John complete his portion of the assignment. The teacher remembered, "I told John quietly but firmly, 'quit your cursing and get to work' but instead of doing what I asked, he yelled at me and then stormed out of the classroom. He slammed the door in one final act of defiance. Both his insubordination and his leaving class without permission were in direct violation of the school's stated policy so I wrote up the appropriate discipline referral and sent it on to the assistant principal. All of this was standard administrative procedure in such cases."

Later that afternoon, the teacher reported he "was called down to the assistant principal's office and I was directed to sit next to John. We were then each asked to present 'our' sides of the story. I was absolutely furious. To me, this was a cut and dried case—the boy was profane, insubordinate, and he left class without permission. The issue should have been resolved by simply deciding on how much punishment to give the boy."

Although the school's official handbook authorized the principal to take "appropriate action, up to and including removal from the school [students] who disrupt the educational process," John received no tangible punishment, only a warning. The next day, he triumphantly returned to the classroom, the clear victor. The administration later tried to accommodate John and his temper by authorizing him to leave any of his classes whenever he felt angry for a so-called "cooling off" period. This, it was hoped, would eliminate confrontations with his teachers. "The one lesson John learned that year," the teacher claimed, "was that it is ok to exhibit whatever behavior you want because the school would not take any substantive disciplinary action. Two years later, he viciously assaulted another boy in the hallway and beat him senseless. I guess he learned this lesson pretty well."

A principal's lack of support for teachers in disciplinary matters quickly alienates a faculty and inevitably intrudes into daily classroom instruction. Some principals will intervene against a teacher even if only one parent calls to complain about a grade or a lesson or an assignment. Teachers are often ordered to grant "special" extensions, provide additional makeup work, and even to exempt students from assignments regardless of their classroom standards and course requirements. Even transcripts, the school's official and final academic record of student progress, can be altered indiscriminately by an unethical principal without an instructor's knowledge or consent.

"Carlos Gomez" was a powerful 5'11", 210-pound tackle who anchored the right side of the offensive line of his high school football team. The boy's long history of poor attendance and erratic behavior led to open speculation about potential drug abuse. Although a native speaker, he was enrolled in a 4th year Advanced Placement Spanish language class. In the spring of his sophomore year, Carlos cut his scheduled Spanish final and then forfeited an additional opportunity to take a make-up test when he failed to appear during the scheduled period. The teacher assigned an *F* for the year, satisfied that she had done all that could be reasonably expected.

When summer football practice began in early August, however, Carlos was an enthusiastic and active participant, despite being clearly ineligible and in direct violation of the state's stringent athletic rules. Two weeks later, when teachers returned for several days of meetings, the principal privately approached the teacher and confided, "We have to save Carlos Gomez. He is a high-risk kid and he needs to take the exam he missed last spring." The teacher was absolutely stunned since in her 18 years of experience, no one had ever so boldly challenged a grade. She adamantly defended the *F* countering that Carlos had had his opportunities and that it wouldn't be fair to less athletically gifted students to make an exception and administer a test fully three months after the exam period. The principal ordered flatly, "I want it done."

The teacher reluctantly complied with the principal's mandate and the exam was given. Because of his native language ability, Carlos passed the test and his final grade was raised to an acceptable mark. As word of the special test leaked out, however, the entire faculty was angry and embittered, sensing that such unwarranted intervention on the part of the principal and the athletic department challenged the entire staff's professionalism and academic integrity. Several weeks later, an anonymous source contacted the local newspaper and informed a reporter of all that had transpired that fall. After several inquiries by the paper, it was "discovered" by the coaching staff that Carlos was still academically ineligible since he had not yet passed the required number of courses to play football, despite the new Spanish grade. The fraud forced the high school's football team to forfeit all six games they had played that season. Even more disastrous was the principal's irreparable loss of credibility and the damage done to the school's reputation for academic integrity. Such actions, even undertaken with the best of intentions, have catastrophic consequences.

A principal's management style, likewise, can have an adverse effect on a school, especially when policy is set by administrative whim with little rationale or faculty input. In such cases, personnel who dare to disagree with the administration are denounced as not being "team players" and even constructive criticism may not be tolerated. Offending faculty members are encouraged to transfer to be replaced by new cronies personally selected by the principal in an effort to build a personal domain.

At one high school in suburban Washington, D.C., when the faculty found their new principal arbitrary, petty, and egocentric, many of the school's most talented and innovative instructors left the school, transferring to more humane and hospitable environments. The students, unfortunately, had no such recourse and were forced to endure each new wave of tyranny as it was thrust upon them. One typical directive prohibited students from staying after school unless under the direct supervision of a teacher. To enforce the rule, so called

"SWAT Teams" roamed the halls, apprehending offending students and herding them into a centralized study hall to await late buses or rides home. One former student recalled that a year after graduation she returned to request a transcript but was accosted by the principal who berated her for cutting classes and threatened immediate suspension. It took several minutes before she could finally convince him that she was no longer a student and hence not subject to his tyranny.

The result of such insensitive management was the destruction of a once positive learning environment. Students quickly complained that the school had become a prison and teachers became increasingly angry and resentful. The faculty lounges were filled with frustration and complaints while some teachers simply chose to avoid the situation by regularly calling in sick. Remarkably, such tyrannical principals are oblivious to the chaos and disorder they inflict, protected by loyal assistants who never dare utter a word of disagreement or criticism and an entrenched bureaucracy that seldom punishes one of their own.

The single most important function of a high school principal is to establish a viable school climate which is physically safe for students and staff while being conducive to learning. If students are consistently truant, classrooms in disrepair, and discipline nonexistent, little can be taught successfully and the school's environment degenerates into chaos. One administrator explained, "I have to give teachers a safe, orderly room—an environment where they can teach. How can you possibly blame a teacher when half the kids are in the hallway and the other half in the classrooms are loaded [on drugs]?"

In recent years, principals have had to confront the persistent problem of physical violence. Fights over drugs, girl friends, and even tennis shoes erupt in school hallways and corridors. Likewise, according to a recently published study by the Institute for the Advancement of Ethics, physical attacks against teachers by students have increased a staggering 700 percent since 1978. In New York City public schools alone, there were over 5,000 reported cases of violence, ranging from battery to rape, against faculty members in 1989. Yet such intolerable conditions are, by no means, confined to eastern urban settings. A teacher in Kansas told researchers with the Carnegie Institute, "Gangs, guns, disruptive behavior . . . spill over into the school [and] have thwarted the ambitious plans to 'reform' education. Within the past two weeks, two of our students have died violently and another is in a hospital recovering from gunshot wounds. Earlier this semester, school was disrupted by a series of fights among rival gangs. I was myself accosted but not harmed by members of [a gang] as I went to the office to sign out for the day." Another teacher from West Virginia in the same report confided, ". . . since becoming a teacher I have had my windshield broken, my tires cut, have been verbally abused by parents, students, and my principal."

A dynamic principal can still transform a school regardless of how ghastly the conditions. During the early eighties, Dr. Henry Gradillas inherited a situation many would have considered hopeless when he assumed the principalship of Garfield High School—later featured in the film *Stand and Deliver*. Located in Los Angeles, the school drew the vast majority of its population from the city's impoverished *barrios*. Of the 3,000 students who attended classes there, many dropped out, while those who graduated rarely went on to college. Most were consigned to a life of menial jobs or manual labor. The school's grounds were desecrated by graffiti and vandalism, student gangs roamed the halls rather than attend class, and hoodlums intimidated and threatened other students.

Henry Gradillas, who had once taught mathematics at the school, took a quick assessment of the situation and deemed it intolerable. He first insisted that students attend the classes they were assigned and strategically posted guards and teachers in the hallways. Those students still caught out of class were assigned a one hour after-school detention period, an assemblage that sometimes numbered over 300 students.

Next, the physical conditions of the building had to be improved. Custodial staff was ordered to remove all graffiti and classroom repairs were mandated. The student restrooms, however, remained the most persistent problem since they had become a haven for various gangs who used the area to play cards, extort money, and sell illicit drugs. Few students even dared use the bathrooms during the school day and most had to be locked because they were inoperable. Gradillas remembers, "The girl's restrooms were atrocious. Half had to be locked because they were so vandalized and destroyed . . . and the very few that were open for girls weren't operable. They had ripped off the doors [to the stalls], there were no toilet paper holders . . . Kids used to bring their own toilet paper to school! Urine was all over the place. Mirrors were long gone. The gangs controlled the restrooms and they would eat there, play cards there, play dice. There were fights and stabbings. Most students wouldn't go to the restrooms but had to wait until they got home to go."

For years, such student misbehavior had been either tolerated by various administrations or the punishments imposed failed to have the deterrent effect. Gradillas discovered that fully 80 percent of Garfield's problems stemmed from three infractions: narcotics, weapons, and fighting. Thus, the elimination of these things became his highest priority. "We were not going to tolerate the three *Ave Maria's,* the three Hail Mary's," Gradillas remembers. "These were the three things that if you got involved with them, you died. If I could eliminate just those three things, I could eliminate 80 percent of the problems at Garfield High School. . . . The power was there but it was never used by the previous principals. For instance, if a kid brought a knife to school, the principal could make a decision as to what was to happen. The toughest penalty was arrest but the most lenient was [peer counseling]. But the kids would laugh at it. . . . The school had a law if you bring a knife to school, the punishment given depends upon the knife. A 3-inch blade or longer you get this, if it is only 2-inches you get that. If a knife was honed on one end or if it was a switch-blade or if it was a bayonet, you get this. In other words, there were ten to twelve definitions of a knife based upon its length and sharpness or how it worked. This would determine the number of days of suspension or whatever. I said, 'this is so sick.' I said to the staff, 'This is out. From now on, we have only one criteria: anything that can be used as a weapon that a student has no use for whatsoever in school and was brought with him, will be looked upon as a weapon and it will mean immediate arrest. Expulsion charges will go out within 24 hours.' "

Since such offenses were in direct violation of the school district's expressed policy as well as California state law, Gra-dillas decided to use the maximum punishments allowed to rid the school of juvenile delinquents and individuals who had no desire to learn. Before implementation of the new policies, the entire student body was informed of the future conse-quences of continued misbehavior. "Why did [principals] have to use the least punishments?" Gradillas wonders. "I used the most. And so when the [student offenders] looked at me and said, 'You are arresting me for a fight?' I said, 'Yes. That is assault and battery with attempt to commit bodily harm. That is a penal code violation, an arrestable offense, a suspendable offense, and an expulsion offense.' And, of course, they would tell me that I didn't have to do that. I could call the parents in and sit down and have a pow wow—that was the minimum. But I could arrest and incarcerate [and that is what I did]. All of those violations the kids thought were rules established by Gradillas. I was given credit for every blasted rule in the school . . . I did not make them but I enforced them."

In the course of a few short years, Garfield had the lowest suspension rate of any school in the entire Los Angeles area.

Gradillas credits this phenomenon to the fact that the school's discipline policy was firm, consistent, and well-known. The student body was aware of the boundaries of appropriate behavior and adapted to the rules.

As the physical condition of Garfield improved, Gradillas made instruction a priority. With only 10 percent of the school's graduates pursuing any form of higher education, it was clear that major changes in the curriculum were vital. He ordered the counselors to encourage all students to accept the academic challenge of higher mathematics to improve their chances of going on to college or obtaining a well paying job, but there was strong resistance. After a year of little progress, Gradillas "personally got a marker, a highlighter, and wiped out 12 classes that were scheduled to be remedial math—basic classes. I said, 'by the power vested in me, these 12 classes we are programming for next year are gone. They don't exist.' And I pencilled in Algebra. The guidance counselors died. Twelve sections of Algebra replacing 12 sections of basic nothing . . . and so they said, 'You're nuts! You are not going to do that.' And I said, 'Yes, it is done. By the power vested in me. It is arbitrary and unilateral. This is not negotiable. This is it.' "

The students were all rescheduled and most were angry when the year began and they were placed in academic track classes. But Gradillas was unyielding, "They cried, screamed, and yelled—they brought in their mothers. And for the next two or three months we had chaos in that school. And I said, 'I am sorry but I will not kick a kid out of there. You stay in there . . . these are the things that have to be done.' We went from one chemistry class to 17 in four years. It was something that hadn't been done in the history of that school. All we did, and the whole basic philosophy of mine is that you treat the kid as if he were your own child by giving him those courses that will enable him to either go to college or into a good paying job or to technical college which will eventually get him a good paying job. If a student is having difficulty in these courses, then we have to kick in support services temporarily to boost him up so he won't fail the class."

The large Latino parent community was encouraged to assist in their children's education, but many were initially intimidated because they lacked even a minimal education. Gradillas still insisted upon their help. "Some of these parents don't have the education. They never went to high school let alone college. They said, 'I can't help my kid in this grade. I don't know anything about science.' So they said it lets us off the hook. And I said, 'Wrong! You can still work with these kids. You can still work and support the school by having the kids do their homework. It's 9 o'clock right now and your girl's outside parked with some guy and she's been out there for two hours. You don't need a PhD to know that she should be at home studying.'

"Kids are watching eight or nine hours of television a day. They start in the morning, they don't come to school, they stay up all night and then they come to school all sleepy because they have been up watching the late show. Parents can stop that. They can stop the telephone. Students don't have to be on the phone. They would be on the phone 24 hours a day [if they could]."

Even with all these efforts, many students were cleverly intercepting teacher progress reports mailed directly to the parents. This effectively kept their parents unaware of their child's daily attendance and academic grades because most of the community's parents had to work and were generally unavailable by telephone during the school day. Gradillas came up with an innovative method of conveying the school's concerns, "I got 4,000 windowed envelopes donated from the Sears stores. I was able to put the information I wanted in there." Without the school's return address on the envelope, the students mistook the letters for a bill. For the first time, the reports reached the parents. "Talk about parental involvement! There was stuff happening in that school that you wouldn't believe. And those kids were mad! But we are the professionals—we are going to have to find ways, any way possible, to teach those kids and you know, the parents will back you."

During the tenure of Henry Gradillas, Garfield High School underwent a remarkable transformation. The school became a center of learning with students finally seeing success in their academic endeavors. It was not without hard work or pain since many of the students had language difficulties and came from a poor socio-economic background. Still, Gradillas insisted that they achieve. He told them, "We are going to extend the school day. We are going to extend the school week. We are going to come in on Saturdays. We are going to come in on Sunday if need be, and on Holy Days of Obligation. In three years, we had 800 kids coming in on Saturdays and we had over 2,000 signing up for summer school of which maybe 1,600 completed more than one course for credit." In the span of just a few years, Garfield High School was administering over 500 advanced placement exams and, in Gradillas's words, "it is still a Latino school in poverty. The students are still brown, still Roman Catholic, and still poor."

The immense and unqualified trust that is placed upon a school principal designates him as the individual most responsible for what happens in a school on a daily basis. Parents entrust their children to a school and have the right to demand a safe and challenging academic environment in which their offspring can learn and grow. Teachers and school boards likewise are entitled to expect inspirational leadership and academic guidance. All parties involved desire fair, firm, compassionate direction. Yet far too many administrators in America either ignore or disregard this sacred trust and refuse to accept the challenge of excellence, content instead with the safe path of mediocrity. This is a betrayal of America's youth who depend upon the schools to prepare them for life in the real world. According to former Secretary of Education, William Bennett, "Good schools have good principals—leaders who articulate clear goals, leaders who show the ability and authority necessary to get teachers and students working together. At present, good principals are far too rare. Too many of our principals are ill-trained as leaders . . . too many avoid initiative and risk-taking." Dr. Henry Gradillas strongly agrees with such an assessment claiming, "We've done all of the reports and all of the surveys, all of the in-services, all of the committees. It is time to move. We know as much about what we should be doing as we are going to know. We should go out there and begin work. I see a lack of leadership in education today. . . . As the principal, I was in a position legally, morally to do something. The principal has the power. Too many in this country, though, have lost it because they refuse to use it. They say, 'I don't have the superintendent's blessing.' You don't need a blessing. Bless yourself and go! It's your job."

Chapter
Three

Who's In

Charge?

"I doubt that I could teach in a modern school, and for good reason. In my day parents and administrators both supported my efforts to be the best teacher possible; today it seems that teachers are not supported by anyone, and I doubt that I could fight undefended."

JAMES MICHENER

THE PUBLIC SCHOOLS WERE ONCE a place where American children went to learn the "Golden Rule" from their teachers. Yet rules have little meaning in today's schools as teachers find increased difficulty in enforcing regulations or compelling adherence to a set of behavioral standards. The simple but tragic fact is that over the past two decades teachers have seen their authority gradually erode and now find themselves no longer in control of their classrooms. The command of the school day has passed from the teacher to the parents, bureaucrats, administrators, and even students, as educators futilely attempt to instruct their pupils in settings over which they have little or no power. The voice of the teacher has little credence and teachers are no longer respected as experts in subject matter or proper student behavior. As a result of this erosion of control, the schools are losing all too many good teachers.

Teachers are professionals attempting to function as specialists in an atmosphere in which they have neither authority nor power commensurate with their expertise. The lawyer is not advised in the law by his clients, nor does the patient dictate medical procedure to his physician. Yet teachers are consistently questioned, advised, and even ignored as they strive to execute their duties in a responsible manner. The American public, in general, presumes to know better than professional educators exactly what needs to take place in the classroom to facilitate learning.

A U.S. Department of Education survey showed that fully 87 percent of all elementary and secondary school teachers reported that disruptive classroom behavior is a major problem in their schools. Of those surveyed, 44 percent believed that such inappropriate student behavior has increased substantially during the past five years. Teachers feel frustrated and handicapped in their own classrooms as they attempt to teach the well-behaved and motivated students, while at the same time attempting futilely to control the obstreperous ones. Many times the best lesson plans are never utilized as the teacher must spend too large a part of instructional time dealing with disruptive students. Good and marginal students suffer and are often sacrificed in systems where problem students are rarely, if ever, removed from the classroom. Little concern is given to the overall impact that youthful hooligans wreak upon the average classroom learning environment or to the emotional harm they freely and indiscriminately inflict upon other students.

Many teachers feel that administrators are out of touch with the problems in the classroom and sometimes totally unresponsive to the need for support felt by the teacher. The responses from administrators confronted with classroom disruptions can range from "there is very little we can do," to "you must be doing something wrong." One teacher confided that her confidence and morale were completely destroyed by an administrator who assumed the teacher was at fault whenever she disciplined a student. The principal repeatedly questioned her judgement and undermined her authority. "I was never called down to the principal's office until I was a teacher," she remarked.

A single, determined, disruptive student can quickly contaminate even the best learning environment and adversely affect the education of the other students by denying them their lawful opportunity to learn. One English teacher said, "The power of a few students when the bad behavior feeds off other bad behavior is not arithmetic, it is geometric. You could light the whole city of New York with the power some students have to control a classroom." Teachers are left feeling frustrated and angry over the system's inability to discipline such unruly students and often yearn for a return to the nostalgic past when few questioned their authority or begrudged them simple respect. "I promised myself that I would never be the teacher who looked back and said, 'I remember when kids acted better,' but things have changed," said a teacher.

The schools of the early sixties were, indeed, vastly different. They were usually governed by a forceful principal who represented a much feared centralized authority in the school. Teachers were, at least outwardly, accorded respect by their students and few dared question either their teaching methods or judgment. Nancy Powell, the principal of Bethesda-Chevy Chase High School, remembered that during her early years as an English teacher, "when kids walked into the classroom in September, they assumed that what you were doing was worthwhile . . . that if they didn't get anything out of it, it was their fault. That was what people believed about the schools. I don't think this was consciously transmitted, but that is the way it was . . . [in the seventies] students walked into your class knowing that your English or history class would be boring, irrelevant. So then the teacher was on the spot to prove to them that the class was both interesting and challenging."

Rules were the cornerstone of education with the schools exerting their authority as *in loco parentis*. Students were forbidden to question such administrative fiats but were expected to quietly comply no matter how arbitrary or trivial the rules may have been. Every aspect of a student's behavior was carefully governed from hair length to dress styles. One typical student handbook commanded, "The overall appearance of every student should be neat." This was defined for boys as the wearing of slacks and collared dress shirts since "t-shirts or sweat shirts, or jeans are not considered appropriate." Boys were also forbidden from growing mustaches, beards, or goatees despite the reality that few high school students were capable of such Herculean feats. For girls, cosmetics were allowed only in "modest proportions," while slacks, pants, and shorts were absolutely forbidden regardless of the weather or temperature. Their dresses or skirts, likewise, had to "be of sufficient size and length and of such material as to avoid any definition or exposure which could be considered inappropriate."

Although such strict control enabled teaching to take place virtually unhindered by behavioral disruptions, such rigid rules left much room for abuse. To most, the schools seemed orderly and peaceful. Frequently, however, they harbored petty bigots and classroom tyrants who used the school's rules to terrorize students. Some male administrators drew perverse pleasure from strict enforcement of the dress codes by crudely running their finger up the back of a girl's blouse to check for bras. One school in Pennsylvania had even adopted an unofficial but crude measurement called "the jiggle factor." In the classroom, a rigid discipline was imposed where the students were expected to sit passively in their seats and absorb a lesson. There were few opportunities for personal expression or individuality or innovative teaching methods.

As the Vietnam War escalated and the nation's cities erupted in social unrest, the artificial tranquility and complacency of the schools abruptly ended. In Des Moines, Iowa, five public schools students including John and Mary Beth Tinker, decided to express their political opposition to American involvement in the Vietnam War by wearing black arm bands to school. The administration claimed that such an exhibition was disruptive to the school's educational climate and quickly responded by suspending all of the participating students.

A court case ultimately ensued and in 1969 reached the United States Supreme Court. In *Tinker vs. Des Moines Independent School District* (393 US 503), the judges ruled decisively in behalf of the students arguing that "[students do not] shed their constitutional rights to freedom of speech or expression at the schoolhouse gate." This landmark judgement was seen as applicable to other areas of student expression and behavior as well. The public schools soon abolished dress codes and removed other rules that could be seen as a restriction on personal expression. The liberalization of the school environment, however, directly led students, parents, and even teachers to question the very role and purpose of the public schools and shattered forever the traditional consensus that had historically governed American education. According to Dr. Barry Farber in *Crisis in Education*, "During the late sixties, teachers seemed to be catching flak from all sides. Not only were adults unconstrained in their criticism but so too were many of the students that teachers were working with. The mood of those years generated a rise in student militancy that reached down to the junior and senior high school levels. From November of 1968 through February of 1969, student protests erupted in 348 high schools in thirty-eight states and the District of Columbia. . . . Students were challenging traditional authority relationships and teachers were hardly exempt. Students complained of having their rights violated, of being subject to capricious policies and rules, of being taught irrelevant subjects by conservative teachers in oppressive surroundings. Again, the partial truth of these complaints should not obscure the point that teachers and schools were being made the focus of grievances of every sort and kind, even those that teachers had no direct responsibility for or bearing on."

In the following years, the schools changed radically. Courses were drastically re-written to emphasize relevancy

rather than academic content and became increasingly esoteric. War and Peace, Human Rights, and other themes replaced conventional history while English became a hodgepodge of unconnected lessons ranging from the "poetry" of Jim
Morrison to the folk songs of Bob Dylan. Throughout the country, area school boards approved millions of dollars for con-
struction of new, open schools. Classrooms became learning
centers without either doors or walls in order to provide
greater freedom and to encourage student expression. Attendance policies disappeared, with students allowed to roam the
halls or campus, liberated from authoritarian rules and regulations. According to Mike Carroll, a high school history
teacher in Maryland, "In the seventies we confused liberty
with license. The freedom to learn, however, is not to do what
you damn well please."

As the schools became increasingly lax, the educational establishment seemed to lose all sense of judgement. Schools
attempted to accommodate virtually all student demands
without regard to long term consequences or simple merit.
Special smoking areas were created in the vast majority of
high schools, thereby giving official sanction to a well-documented health risk. Besides the questionable morality of providing 14-year-old tobacco addicts with ample opportunity to
smoke, these student sanctuaries became a place to gather
during classes since few administrators dared venture into
such inhospitable locations. Drug usage correspondingly increased, rising to epidemic levels with the acrid aroma of marijuana providing a regular backdrop to the school day. Open
campuses where students could come and go as they pleased
also contributed to a decrease in decorum. Students came to
their classes stoned, completely unable to participate in class
activities or even comprehend simple instruction. Drugs
quickly became a major source of confrontation between students and teachers. The school had degenerated into a convenient social gathering place rather than an institution of
learning.

During the early eighties, as SAT scores spiraled downward, public high schools responded by attempting to reclaim some of the authority so willingly ceded during the previous decade. Back-to-basics became the rallying cry of reformers in an effort to get schools to tighten up on discipline and get back to the business of more rigorous academic expectations. Unfortunately, the authority and control the schools had given up during the late sixties have not been easy to reclaim. The smoking courts were gradually abolished, gone and unmourned by teachers; walls were hastily built in the open schools to restore the integrity of the classroom; and attendance policies were generally strengthened and enforced. These changes, however, were not enough to regain control, as the schools were no longer dealing with the same types of students or families.

The demographic transformation of the United States has proven to be a far greater obstacle to educational reform. The traditional family structure commonly accepted as the norm in previous years has been fundamentally altered, ravaged by an epidemic of divorces and the resulting growth of single-parent households. According to a 1987 survey conducted by the Department of Commerce, 61 percent of all mothers with school-aged children currently work outside the home, creating, at best, a less nurturing environment for their children. Perhaps the most frightening trend, though, has been the basic change in attitudes toward parenting. According to Secretary William Bennett, "You talk about a cultural shift, [a survey] asked American parents in 1965 what is the priority of children in your life, 85 percent said number one. When they asked in 1985, it had dropped considerably to three or four. All of the teachers I've talked to say that the single most important factor in changing the schools is the parents."

Modern schools, along with their academic responsibilities, have been required to look after the emotional well-being of students. Although many teachers have a close mentoring relationship with certain students, sheer numbers preclude

DOONESBURY copyright 1991 G.B. Trudeau. Reprinted with permission of Universal Press Syndicate. All rights reserved.

such important contact for all. For other students, poor class-room behavior frequently is symptomatic of deeper problems at home. While parents expect and demand that the schools magically take appropriate, corrective action, they too have abandoned the teacher, refusing to accept any responsibility or to reinforce academic expectations in the home.

A popular high school teacher remembered a particularly dramatic case. "We had a problem student who was causing all of her teachers fits. She was arrogant, obnoxious, and fre-quently violent. It was obvious that she was harboring a lot of bitterness and we teachers became the target for most of it.

"The biggest problem was that the girl was completely un-predictable. Some days she would sit quietly in class, put her head down and go to sleep while on other days, an innocent remark would set her off. She would curse, scream, and then walk out of class. Finally, the school's guidance department in desperation arranged for a parent conference between the girl's father and her teachers so we could discuss what had become simply an intolerable situation.

"The meeting turned out to be a real revelation. The father was attempting to raise the girl alone but he had a high-powered, very prestigious job that kept him at work until after 10 o'clock each night so the girl was left home alone. She had no one to talk to, to confide in, or to provide love, let alone anyone who would provide some basic behavioral guidance. Yet the father came to the school wanting to know how the teachers were going to handle the situation and what special strategies we were going to devise to help modify the girl's behavior. It was absolutely incredible and yet none of us dared get up and tell him, 'Hey, we're not miracle workers. Why don't you pay more attention to your kid and establish some basic rules for her to live by.' Parents just don't want to hear those kind of things since it is a lot easier to blame the schools than to admit their own personal shortcomings."

One of the most pressing problems for today's teachers is the lack of power to control their classrooms without interference from outside influences. Often disregarded as the force in charge of the learning situation, the teacher is frequently second-guessed by parents and overruled by administrators. Even if a school administrator takes strong action in the case of a troublemaker, the system frequently frustrates or thwarts the effort. Disciplinary actions are often overturned at the highest level of the school system, rendering school-based personnel impotent. Private and parochial schools rarely experience such problems since high tuition payments by their very nature screen out many uninvolved families. Furthermore, the real threat of expulsion, an option rarely exercised in the public schools, poses a deterrent to extreme behavior. In one typical suburban Catholic intermediate school, an 8th grader was caught with a small amount of marijuana. Since all drugs were clearly forbidden and a detriment to the school's educational mission, there were no second chances. The principal, a no-nonsense Jesuit priest, immediately summoned the parents to the school for a 2 o'clock meeting, at which time he delivered both their son and a refund check for the remaining portion of the semester's tuition. Subsequently, the boy was enrolled in the local public school where administrators and teachers had little power and no such discipline options. Because of state mandated educational guarantees, a similar drug offense would incur only a minor suspension penalty.

Parents who openly profess great concern about their children's educational development but consistently question the professionalism of teachers and their judgment, can do more harm than good. A teacher remembered one such parent who called to angrily attack the county's foreign language program for seventh graders, demanding that in addition to Spanish and French, the school offer Latin since his daughter would need such a strong academic background for her anticipated admission to Harvard in 1997.

Another teacher recounted the story of how a parent of one high school boy not only attempted to control the course content of his son's English class, but also dictated the number of assignments given, as well as providing an on-going critique of the teacher's individual teaching style. Despite the fact that the boy was doing quite well in the course, the parent contended that as a college professor, he was an expert on education and knew better than high school teachers what was needed for university-bound students. He advised the teacher to severely modify her program to include weekly formal, multi-page writing assignments in all classes and that each student assignment be intensely evaluated and returned with extensive written comments. Then, each student could rewrite the paper and make corrections after a personal conference with the teacher. The teacher carefully and diplomatically explained that the reality of a class load of 150 students precluded such exercises on a routine basis. The father then callously proceeded to challenge the school's effectiveness and her commitment to education.

Students, likewise, exhibit an alarming disrespect for teachers and their profession. In their minds, teachers do not merit the respect or obedience they once commanded. Jenny Bastress, a student at the University of Michigan, recalled that in her high school, "Some students today have the attitude, 'I'm better than you. You're just a teacher.' Their goals in terms of high school are to get into an Ivy League College so they can get into a good law school or med school so they can make a lot of money." Caroline Frick, a history major at Miami University of Ohio, agreed maintaining that, "Some students [in high school] were very condescending to teachers . . . they had no respect and would make fun of them."

Students, however, are not the only ones who strip teachers of their authority. A teacher with 12 years experience told of the disastrous combination of lack of respect on the part of the students coupled with no support from the administration. "In one incident I sat down between two boys because one was constantly picking on the other. I asked them to be quiet and, as I seated myself, the bully turned to me and said, 'Just because you are sitting there doesn't mean that I am going to stop talking.' I replied that he would keep talking over my dead body and he replied that he could arrange that too.

"This was one of many things that happened in this class over a period of weeks. I did go to see an administrator early on and she called the boys into her office to talk about it. The students involved were very angry with me for bringing this to the attention of the administration. After that occasion, every time something happened in the class they would say sarcastically, 'Are you afraid that we are going to kill you? You afraid you're going to get raped? You afraid you're going to get murdered?' The idea they had was that I was picking on them because I was afraid of them. What I really wanted was for them to do their work and behave and stop all the fresh-mouthed behavior. I felt that from that point I could do nothing because there was no administrative follow-up and nothing ever happened."

Teachers are increasingly alone, frustrated, and isolated in the modern American high school, surrounded by administrators who refuse to provide much-needed support. An Arizona educator observed, "The administration doesn't want to deal with disruptive students. They have, at our school, a list of five 'interventions' that a teacher must try before they can refer a student to the office. And then they begin to question a teacher's management style rather than the inappropriate behavior. It is the teacher who is left feeling inadequate."

Another veteran teacher said, "I have made myself feel miserable about myself because I feel inadequate in dealing with the extreme problem kids. When you turn to the administrator and say, 'I really need support with this,' you are told they really can't do very much about it. I really felt so inadequate and so miserable that after one really bad situation I was truly on the verge of leaving teaching because I could see no way out of it and I hated feeling that way."

The teacher who justifiably seeks help with unmanageable students is regarded as weak by superiors. Unfairly, the label of incompetence is placed on those who are having classroom management problems due to a quirk of fate that dealt them a disastrous combination of troublemakers and incorrigibles in one class. When the administration glosses over or ignores a difficult situation, or tells teachers that there is very little anyone can do to correct it, they feel there really is no chance for improvement. The confidence and effectiveness of the teachers is diminished as they begin to feel that the problem lies with themselves rather than with the offenders. When teachers are told by administrators that they are part of the problem and that they just have to live with the consequences, the self-esteem of the teachers is destroyed and morale and classroom decorum deteriorate.

This very real abandonment has led many educators to develop simple survival techniques that allow them to exist day-to-day and to operate in inhospitable schools where their authority is either nonexistent or constantly challenged. Conflict avoidance is one of the most common techniques, where belligerent students are not disciplined, classroom doors are locked to avoid hallway violence, and minor infractions of rules are tolerated. In *The Shopping Mall High School*, the authors explain, "One teacher, for example, reported that she acquiesced to a 'cookbook' approach to math rather than one that emphasized 'the whys of it' because she feared students would become 'rebellious' if she stressed the latter. A remedial teacher settled for silence rather than discussions that might cause 'confrontation' because 'as soon as they feel threatened, they lash out.' Not assigning homework was justified on the grounds of avoiding 'behavioral problems,' and not disturbing students who were under the influence of alcohol was tolerated as long as they did not 'get obstreperous.' Going along with kids avoided problems and hassles."

Just as disturbing are the growing numbers of teachers who, in a desperate attempt to solve the dilemma of disruptive students, only succeed in exacerbating the problem as they continually pass unmotivated students so long as they are not disruptive and sit passively in class. These teachers feel they have no power to correct bad situations. Instead of fighting a losing battle with parents or administrators, they make concessions in order to survive the day as best they can. One student explained this unwritten but clear agreement, "I slept most of the time in his class. I didn't even turn in all of the work and I still got a passing grade."

Schools have further ceded their authority by replacing rules with "Student Rights and Responsibilities" (SRR). These elaborate lists extensively detail the school's obligations to its students and, to a lesser degree, define their responsibilities to the school. Such manuals, while properly recognizing the basic Constitutional rights of students, have also increasingly transformed the process of learning into the obligation of the teacher rather than that of the student. "The teacher shall . . ." has replaced "the student will . . ." in such administrative edicts. The unintended but very real result is that students in modern schools are less willing to accept responsibility for their own behavior or even to acknowledge their own important role in their eventual academic success or failure.

Students have at various times been formally guaranteed such student "rights" as mandatory exam review days, special no-homework periods and designated testing days for all subjects. No consideration is ever given to curriculum requirements or instructional realities, nor is any effort made to consult teachers or to accommodate their needs. Instead, such policies are implemented and mandated by people outside the classroom, compelling teacher compliance and further weakening the important autonomy of the classroom teacher.

Students have quickly become experts on their guaranteed rights and continually attempt to hold teachers accountable for any perceived violations. One group of students even went so far as to form a vigilante committee to monitor teacher compliance with the SRR guidelines. During a hot day in the early fall, a math teacher sent a sophomore girl to the office because, much to the delight of the boys in the class, she was wearing an extremely low cut blouse. The teacher deemed that the girl's appearance was inappropriate and disruptive since studying equations proved difficult when confronted with a far more interesting subject.

Later in the day, the student committee visited the teacher during her planning period. Armed with a copy of the SRR handbook, they asked for an explanation of why the girl was removed from class. Some twenty years after Mary Beth Tinker boldly defied school policy for the legitimate right of student political expression, the argument has now degenerated to the merits of a young lady's right to expose her breasts in public.

One teacher recounted how, in her system, Thursdays had been set aside as the specially designated test day for science classes, a test being defined as "any written evaluation lasting in excess of 20 minutes." She explained, "I disagreed with the policy but I honored it even though if there was an assembly or some other modification of the schedule, it could be two weeks before I was allowed to give a unit test. But still, every Friday I continued to give a routine five question vocabulary *quiz*. It was a short and simple assignment that required a minimal amount of study or preparation. I had been doing this for years with no problem or complaints. In fact, most students looked forward to the quizzes because they generally helped improve their grades.

"After the testing policy was initiated, though, one disgruntled student went to the principal and complained that I was testing on a non-science day. Without even consulting me, the next Monday I received a written reprimand from the principal reiterating the testing policy and chastising me for violating it. I was furious and wrote a terse response back saying that I was in compliance with the county's policy and that I resented being checked upon by the 'test police.' But it just goes to show that today a student's word carries greater weight than that of a teacher."

Students do have a great deal of power to manipulate a school situation. An English teacher explained, "We permit kids to call the shots and even when other students perceive that that is not the way to have it happen, they are caught in the middle. In the past two years we have had a tendency to give students a way of dealing with classroom situations that allows them to be disruptive. For example, a student is told by the administrator that any time he feels too much pressure to get up and walk out of the room. Theoretically that is wonderful. You talk to an administrator and they say they want to avoid confrontations between the student and the teacher. I have had two students this year who have had this wonderful privilege. The idea is that the class will return to normal, but this, in fact, does not happen. This happens only in a fantasy world that somebody has concocted."

The decision by someone outside the classroom to bequeath such an option as time-out privileges upon students usurps the power of the teacher. Furthermore, the administrators who call for such a practice, often have scant knowledge or understanding of the impact felt in the classroom. They are simply not there to see the effect these types of policies have on the teacher and other students. A teacher explained, "The students are in charge and they can call all the shots. Administrators want to make it easier for the students so that they do not get involved in more problems when they should clearly be held accountable for their actions."

Another disciplinary action commonly used in school is suspension of miscreants for a short period of time. No grade penalty is imposed for missing school because it is illegal for schools to impose academic penalties for discipline. Unless the parents exact some kind of punishment at home, the student is, in effect, given a school-mandated vacation. Students with recurring behavior problems do not want to be in school anyway, and the school is actually rewarding them for their bad behavior by giving them a few days off. Teachers must provide make-up work and extra help for those offending students when they return, adding to the teachers' already huge workload.

A teacher said, "The student is out of school on suspension with an approved absence and the teacher is punished by being responsible for helping him to make up the work he has missed. The student is the one who has been at fault and now he is being rewarded. There is no penalty for the student who is suspended. He is getting a free day off. It is absolutely mind-boggling. I wish they would suspend me so that I could have a few days off."

Teachers no longer command the respect or wield the authority they once did in American public school systems. No matter how hard teachers work, and in fact most of them do commit themselves to doing a good job in their profession, today's teachers are not given the power they once were to successfully manage their domain. Until the opinions of students, parents, and society change concerning the authoritative role of the teacher, America's schools will remain mired in mediocrity. If the commonly heard lament, "There is nothing we can do about it," is not silenced soon, the quality of education available to students will remain mired in mediocrity and teachers will continue to be stranded in chaotic school situations where others are in charge.

Chapter
Four

The

Front Lines

"More is demanded of a high school teacher than a college teacher. You have to take on so many different roles. . . . There are so many other pressures besides just teaching."

CAROLINE FRICK
STUDENT

AMERICANS COMMONLY PERCEIVE the teaching profession as an attractive occupation. They envision a career in which an individual works merely nine months a year, approximately seven hours a day, with summers and holidays free from responsibility. Missing from this conception is an understanding of the numerous components that contribute to a competent teacher's professional life. A teacher's year starts before the students arrive and ends after they depart, creating an actual ten-month school year, with the two summer months anything but idle. Summers are filled with advanced course work, as teachers are required by various regulations to remain certified in their subject matter. Study in preparation for the upcoming school year and college course work or summer school teaching easily fills that time. Many teachers devote precious summer weeks to attending sports camps, yearbook and newspaper workshops, pre-season sports training sessions, special study programs, or musical and drama workshops with students, all without financial remuneration. Holidays are used for grading student papers, writing college recommendation letters, or averaging grades for upcoming report cards.

Likewise, the teacher's work schedule is not the seven-hour day commonly accepted by the public. Successful teachers enter the school early to organize for the day's lessons and leave hours after the actual school day ends. Student conferences, departmental or faculty meetings, sports practices or extra-curricular activities all occur after classes end and would not exist at all without teacher commitment. Frequently the only time a teacher is able to prepare materials or grade papers is during non-contractual hours. Most teachers spend many hours at home on phone calls, class preparation and paper-work. It is not uncommon for a teacher to leave school after a ten-hour day only to return to school for an evening event. The unseen efforts that contribute to the time spent in class-room teaching accumulate quickly, creating an actual work week of 50 to 60 hours instead of the misconceived 35-hour week.

Gary Sykes writes in *Restructuring Schools,* "[Teachers] often compare themselves to physicians in battlefields, under fire, lacking medical supplies, overwhelmed by the number of casualties pouring in. They resort to triage techniques simply to cope. But the difference, for teachers, is that these are normal or typical conditions of their work, not rare or extraor-dinary circumstances."

Teachers, unlike other professionals, have no offices, no phones and little, if any, clerical help. Even those teachers with the benefit of phones have no private phone, and often serve as secretaries for other department members, contin-ually taking and running telephone messages to their col-leagues. Other teachers must spend their precious time wash-ing student graffiti off desktops, washing chalkboards, and doing basic secretarial work. Teachers must allocate time each day for standing in line to use the school's copying machine. Horror stories abound about how tests must be rescheduled and lessons postponed because of difficulties with copying. One teacher complained, "I can't tell you how many times I've had to modify my class because the copy machine was broken down or because ten other teachers were in line in front of me. Even when I can get the copying done, it often is of such poor quality that it negates all the time I put into developing the lesson. The sad fact is that education is ten years behind the rest of society in technology. We get all of the old, obsolete equipment that businesses no longer want or use." Another teacher lamented that these types of problems are so typical and such a hindrance to performing his job that, "It would almost be worth the money to buy my own copying machine for home so I could count on being prepared every day. It is ridiculous to have to worry about a machine. We're here to worry about the kids." Advance planning takes care of the copying problems, but spontaneity is lost as the teacher can never count on being able to produce a class-set for any activity that may be sparked by inspiration, current events, or the immediately preceding lesson.

Managers in the private sector would be hard-pressed to function effectively without a profusion of technical aids to facilitate the running of an efficient business. Even the small business could not exist without typewriters, computers, copying machines, fax machines, telephones and clerical support. A company today would quickly fail if these vital technical resources were not available. Yet the teacher deals daily with the lack of technical and clerical support which drastically cuts down efficiency and effectiveness. Time is wasted by the teacher who must first find a private telephone before making a necessary professional call. The teacher without an office is forced to prepare or grade papers in the school library or faculty lounge, neither very conducive to concentration. Tasks then take two to three times as long to complete due to the unprofessional working conditions that exist in most schools.

Planning time does exist and is crucial to teachers. It is a sacred period during the day, provided for educators to prepare lessons, grade papers, research the topics to be taught, and to complete various other pressing tasks. Most secondary teachers are assigned to teach a set number of classes, and are also provided with at least one 'free' period, often less than an hour, in which they can attend to their schoolwork.

Despite persistent teacher complaints, school boards are reluctant to grant additional planning time to educators due to budgetary constraints and the desire to schedule as many classes as possible with the allotted staff. Teachers are thus expected to promptly grade student papers, organize assignments, and prepare for classes during non-working hours while balancing the additional duties routinely assigned such as bus duty, cafeteria monitoring, and study halls.

The planning period may, however, unexpectedly disappear from a teacher's day for various reasons as the needs of the entire school must be met. Substitute teachers are routinely hired to fill in for absent educators, yet frequently, adequate subs cannot be found to cover all classes. Students cannot go unsupervised, so teachers are called on to oversee extra classes. Teachers also may be called on by their colleagues to teach their classes so that they may attend a professional meeting or attend to another work-related event only available to them if they can find their own coverage. Not an infrequent occurrence, the unexpected loss of planning time infringes on the effectiveness of the teacher called upon to cover in an emergency.

The accumulation of even the small problems of the day interfere just as profoundly with the day's instruction. Shortages of basic clerical supplies may seem like a minor problem, but when such items are crucial to the execution of one's job, they become paramount. One teacher revealed that she once had been forced to wait two weeks for much-needed overhead transparencies for use in her classroom. Another was told that even chalk had to be conserved because the supply was low. Paper for duplicating was also rationed until the school's allocation could be filled from a central warehouse, yet when the shipment arrived, the copying machines were all broken. The teachers had to wait and make do. Study questions could be hastily written on the blackboard, but a major test could not be given that way, and students who had been repeatedly told to be organized and work according to schedule were delighted to see that the school itself could not function in such an efficient manner. Teachers are constantly exhorted to display creative and innovative methods of teaching in the attempt to be more effective educators. Instruction can be provided without high-tech equipment, yet teachers then are reprimanded for not being current in their instructional methods. If high-tech teaching is required, then the high-tech world must be accessible to the classroom teacher.

As innovative teachers try to vary instruction and motivate students, many depend upon audio-visual equipment and other materials that are frequently in need of repair. Such repairs must be authorized by a central bureaucrat in a distant office who may not be aware of, or concerned about, the immediacy of the problem. An elusive, over-worked repairman may then not be able to make essential repairs for several months.

In tough budgetary times, teachers can function without some of the frills and gadgets, but no school can function without books. In some schools, even books cannot be found in adequate supply to meet the basic needs of the teachers or students. Consequently, students are forced to share books or read poorly and illegally reproduced copies of the chapters, all of which put an additional burden on the teacher while limiting the amount of material taught to the students.

The public is unaware of what teachers really confront in their schools each day, uninformed about how much time a teacher needs to prepare a lesson and about the percentage of time a teacher is actually able to teach. In response to the query, "What did you do in school today?" countless parents receive the pat response, "Nothing." All too often that assessment of the day's learning is woefully accurate, not due to the lack of talented teachers or their desire to teach, but as a direct result of too much to do, insufficient time to do it, and increasing intrusions on teaching time.

The average 45-minute class period can be quickly eroded to only one-half hour or less of instructional time as the teacher must deal with numerous other tasks. Students must be seated, attendance taken, notes signed, latecomers dealt with, papers collected or returned, announcements made and extraneous questions answered. On an ideal day, such routine duties can be executed in five or six minutes, but in dealing with teenagers the unexpected is more often the norm. A recalcitrant student, a fight between classmates, or the collective mood of a class can erase even more time that should be spent on subject matter. Seemingly inconsequential occurrences like a student's coughing fit, snow falling outside the window, or a bumblebee circling the room can consume class time. Current events can supersede school matters. The reality is that these issues must be examined and handled before the lesson can start. Such a fast-paced, unpredictable atmosphere requires attention that is then not spent on teaching.

The frustration of countless hectic hours spent at school with very little teaching accomplished plagues many a teacher. Many peripheral duties and concerns have crept into the daily running of a school, and no matter how necessary these functions may be, they detract drastically from the actual quantity and quality of instruction.

The overwhelming drain that a teaching career has on an individual leaves teachers understandably demoralized. A recent study of all teachers say they tend to subordinate all other aspects of their lives to their work as a teacher. Thirty-seven percent of all teachers admit they work 50 hours or more a week on their job, yet only half of that time is spent in actual instruction. The work load of today's teacher is enormous, and the problems and issues that must be confronted in the classroom before any teaching can even take place have increased drastically over the past decade.

The "front lines" of today's high schools are a turbulent and difficult place to work. John Sculley, Chairman, President and CEO of Apple Computer, Inc., writes in a current advertisement, "We expect our teachers to handle teenage pregnancy, substance abuse, and the failings of the family. Then we expect them to educate our children." Not only are these topics on the agenda of most high schools, AIDS, racial awareness, societal violence, child abuse, and a vast array of other social problems must also be dealt with.

Many teachers find themselves functioning out of necessity as counselors or social workers. In a Carnegie Institute study on education, one secondary teacher from Illinois described the issues confronting educators in modern classrooms, "Most 'news' articles on the state of education fail to take into account the complexity of the problem, negative aspects of our culture or the effects of poor family relationships on student performance. It is easier to blame the teachers for all the problems. Currently seven of my students' parents (maybe more) are getting divorces. One stepfather raped his daughter; two girls told me of sexual abuse when they were young; one boy killed himself; two boys related to me of suicide attempts; one girl ran away to Florida for two months and now has a child; one got pregnant, had an abortion (last year) and now has a two-week-old child. Other children face difficulties of a dying parent. Drinking at home by parents and children is a problem."

Many factors come into play as teachers futilely try to attend to the business of each day. Teachers feel that instruction is the last priority on the educational agenda. One teacher, a veteran of 30 years said, "There are a lot more interruptions in the course of a week or semester than there ever used to be, so a lot less time is spent on the subject matter. Teaching is the least important part of our day now."

One would think that once the teacher is in the classroom, the job would be easy. The door closes and the teacher does what he has been trained for—teaches. Teaching would be

© 1991 United Feature Syndicate, Inc.

PEANUTS. Reprinted by permission of UFS, Inc.

rewarding and enjoyable, if it could take place with minimal interruption, but at times even seemingly beneficial activities can harm the educational process in unexpected ways. Students involved in athletics, music, drama and interscholastic activities can cause countless breaks in a teaching day, especially during the most active sports seasons of fall and spring. Frequently, students must leave school as early as noon on the day of an event in order to travel to a rival school. In rural districts where the distance is greater, students may leave even earlier. Some miss afternoon classes once or twice a week, a significant loss of teaching time when multiplied by the number of weeks in a season. Even worse is the class with numerous athletes on different teams, where anywhere from five to fifteen students are missing on the same day for tennis, soccer, cross country, girl's field hockey, football, or golf, all competing in the same season. Even if the students are hardworking and dedicated and make up the work missed, the teacher is faced with the extra duty of creating and administering make-up tests, and dealing with partial classes left behind who often adopt the attitude, "Nobody's here today so why do we have to work?" Planning class presentations and group work can be disastrous since it is virtually impossible to assemble an entire group. Classroom lectures and discussions never become part of the absent athlete's educational experience. High school courses cannot be reduced to correspondence courses. Discussions, where the exchange of ideas and learning takes place, are an integral part of the school process that is lost forever. The effect of such disruption is felt by all the students, not just those attending outside events. No new subjects are introduced because the material must be re-taught to those absentees and the class may be put on hold for the day. Even though the remaining students are in class, all suffer from the absence of so many.

A relatively recent phenomenon has been the encouragement by admissions offices throughout the country for high school seniors to make visits to prospective colleges. Each week during the fall semester, high school classes are depleted by long weekend visits by high school seniors to colleges and universities. Previewing the schools prior to application for admission is now no longer adequate. Students, often accepted by more than one college, then choose to re-visit in order to make their final decision. These spring trips are, in fact, little more than an excuse to enjoy the various social amenities of collegiate life and to further the pervasive feeling that their senior year is a time of frolic and frivolity. For 12th grade teachers, the scheduling of tests or major projects takes on nightmarish proportions when trying to adjust work around the travel plans of their students. In classes with mixed grade levels, the underclassmen are left in a disrupted situation in which the normal business of the day cannot take place. Once again, all students are harmed. The negative impact need never be felt if the students had only been in class in the first place.

Regardless of the necessity or validity of some disruptions, educators cannot help but feel discouraged as they attempt to provide quality lessons covering an ever-growing body of information to an increasingly absent student audience. In this environment it is not surprising that student absenteeism is all too common. A recent educational study reported that 31 percent of secondary school teachers believe that absenteeism is a serious problem in the public schools, compared to just 18 percent in 1987. One Wisconsin teacher stated in *The Condition of Teaching,* "The truancy rate continues to rise as there is no one to monitor whether children go to school or not. . . . It appears that education isn't as important as people say it is."

Most schools will excuse students from class for such legitimate reasons as illness, a death in the immediate family, a court appearance, or a doctor's appointment. The reason for the absence is provided on a note from a parent requesting the school to excuse the child. But in actuality, many students stay away from school for a variety of other reasons. Some parents will use older siblings for child care if their normal arrangements fall through; others keep a high school student home to meet the repairman or accept a delivery of some kind. A child who is tired from an extracurricular activity, such as a band concert, may be allowed to sleep late in the morning only to show up later in the day with a note that says he was "sick" and had to come to school late. Family vacations take priority over the educational process with parents removing their child for days and later citing illness as an excuse. Compounding the problem are those who play hooky and view cutting a class as a challenge, or who pick and choose which classes to attend based on whether they like the teacher or the subject matter.

Some may argue that the student is only hurting himself, which is simply not true. The absence of these students is a burden on the school and the teacher. The amount of time and paperwork, especially with frequent or long-term absences, is detrimental to the entire educational process. Teachers are obligated to provide make-up work for the student who is absent from class with an excused absence. For those who are ill, or genuinely in need of the work, teachers rarely complain, but, for the increasing number of students who require individual work to go on vacation, or to enjoy the luxury of sleeping late in the morning, the teacher feels abused. Dedicated teachers are misused as they help absent students rather than hard-working, motivated pupils who really need extra help. Parents who are compliant in the abuse of the system compound the problem. If education were truly a priority in American society, the parents would be sure that their children were attending classes. Instead, the message is sent over and over again that school is not important and eventually everyone, teachers included, begins to feel the same.

Teachers have chosen their profession based upon a desire to help young people and to convey their enthusiasm for a subject they love. Despite the problems encountered in education, great satisfaction can be felt through the close interaction with students. The look on the face of the girl who has just discovered a new idea, the pleasure a boy receives from a job well done, can make it all worthwhile. Many excellent, motivated students inhabit the schools, but for each successful youth, there seem to be twice as many who are disinterested. Student apathy is one of the most difficult barriers a teacher faces. Not only does the indifferent student affect the morale of the teacher, he likewise interferes with the education of classmates concerned with learning.

Too many students will not read the books assigned, do not bother to do homework, and refuse to make up any work they have missed. When a significant part of the class is not prepared for the lesson, alterations must be made in the teacher's presentation. Most often this results in the re-teaching or exclusion of certain material in order to fit the time allotted in the semester. Students who are ready to proceed to new material must suffer through unnecessary repetition, thus becoming bored or discouraged. They then adopt the attitude that it doesn't matter if they work either. One secondary history teacher lamented the aversion to work that some of his students displayed and said, "It is frustrating. I guess what they want is for you to give them free time and then give them an A. That's what the students seem to expect." The teacher is made to feel as if the responsibility for learning falls upon the teacher and not the student.

Homework serves various purposes in the instructional process. Reading can serve as a basis for discussion as well as providing a base of information. Written exercises and research activities provide essential reinforcement for a classroom lesson, but it is commonplace in American society for many students to refuse to do work outside of class. Some students fail to do so simply because they do not care, leading 46 percent of secondary school teachers to list student apathy as a serious problem in their schools. Students are required by law to be at school but once they leave the confines of the classroom, monitoring the educational process becomes the responsibility of the parent. A secondary teacher from Wisconsin explains, "Students watch more hours of TV than they spend in school and never read outside of the classroom . . . (parents) are often too tired or guilt-ridden to spend the time necessary to force their children to do homework." Such factors may provide a convenient rationalization, but they cannot exonerate the parents from blame nor excuse them from their responsibilities.

Students likewise have significant responsibility for their own education, but have a variety of excuses for their failure to complete their school work. Lack of time caused by sports activities, drama productions, musical groups, or other extra-curricular activities is one of the most common. Time for studying, they argue, does not exist after they get home, eat, bathe, relax, and go to bed. Motivation for studying is non-existent when they consign higher priority to other, more enjoyable activities.

Another group of students who do few school assignments after hours are those who work at a job. For some, especially among newly arrived immigrants, this is necessary for their own or their family's economic survival. For such students, simply getting to school at all can be extremely difficult, and homework is virtually an impossible task. Other students work to provide money for luxuries such as cars, trendy clothes, or even drugs and alcohol. Whatever the reason, the teacher is left to cope with the problem and is ultimately blamed for the lack of student progress.

With school boards requiring more credits for graduation and class time being eroded by daily disruptions and other non-academic activities, the teacher cannot take the time to allow the students to finish homework in class. Homework is work to be done. When teachers impose an academic penalty for inferior work, central office bureaucrats demand that teachers justify in writing the grades of students receiving D's or F's and it is the teacher who is expected to change. The failure is imposed on the teacher rather than the students.

Pride in doing well seems conspicuously absent from the contemporary classroom. Students seem to pigeonhole knowledge into the setting in which they learned it and see no connection between the disciplines. Some critics say they are lazy while more generous observers may claim they are merely unaware of the benefits schooling could offer them. Students forced to use proper grammar, punctuation and syntax in an English class may turn in an unscholarly mess for a science project. When questioned about the quality of the work, the reply is usually, "What? This isn't English class!" The idea that excellence of performance should be a comprehensive concept is not accepted by most young people.

Even if students are inspired to work, the sheer numbers of students in the classroom can be the final factor to drive a good teacher from the classroom. California and Utah are among the worst examples of classroom overcrowding with over 50 percent of classes consisting of 30 to 39 students. Given the best of circumstances, an excellent teacher with motivated students, there is still a limit to what individual teachers can do. Over-enrolled classes present problems that make effective teaching difficult, if not impossible. In some extremely large classes all seems well. The teacher is competent at classroom management, all is orderly and the students are attentive and motivated. In the classroom, things seem fine, but when the teacher is confronted with the overwhelming numbers of papers generated by the students, both the student and the teacher suffer. Two things can happen. Either the teacher spends large amounts of time grading class assignments, becoming stressed and possibly less effective in the classroom, or very little written work is assigned, leaving the students deficient. Another detriment of such oversized classes is the lack of "air time" for each student. In smaller, more intimate settings, the teacher can come to know the students and draw them out in discussions or work with them personally during class time. In classes of 30 or more, the student suffers from being lost in the crowd. Teachers tend to talk only to those who volunteer in class. In a larger group, it becomes easier for quieter students to simply disappear into the background.

One English teacher on the West Coast started the school year with 186 students. If each of those students were to write just one composition every week, and only 15 minutes was devoted to grading each one, almost 30 non-classroom hours would be spent on grading compositions in a five-day period of time. With all other duties required for effective teaching, this work week could exceed 70 hours.

In better situations in which classes are small and more intimate, a teacher can devote more energy to all aspects of the class. This proves beneficial to both the students and the teacher. In *The Condition of Teaching,* one teacher from Oklahoma explained, "I have manageable classes with 19-23 students each hour. After years of teaching 30+ students per hour, I can see a marked difference in my students' performance in these smaller classes. The classroom atmosphere is relaxed because I can be more relaxed. I have adequate time in class for group instruction and individual tutoring."

With typical teachers assigned five classes per day, in as many as three different courses, mental and physical exhaustion results when a teacher becomes so overloaded with students. He is always behind, always has papers to grade and return, always has work to prepare. Not only do teachers become demoralized by the situation, students also feel discouraged by a situation when their voices are not heard, their papers not read, and their needs not met. They rightly begin to feel like mere numbers. Parents, too, feel that teachers do not know their children and quickly consign blame to teachers, arguing that they just do not care. Placing already overburdened teachers in oversized classes creates a no-win situation for all involved. Teaching quality declines and the potential of the students is not tapped.

Good teachers suffer from their own competency, while those with poor performance and mediocre skills have the best deal. The least effective teachers are free from all of the extra duties necessary to run a comprehensive school program since they are considered to be incompetent in certain areas, but not bad enough to fire. The conscientious, hard-working teachers, however, are the ones who are always asked to assume the added burden by doing a little bit more to help the students. The same core group of individuals in a school is often asked to assume more responsibility because of their obvious dedication to the profession.

Conversely, the less effective teachers do not worry about students or school once the dismissal bell rings. They punch the clock and go on with their own personal lives, while their more involved colleagues finish the day exhausted and facing hours of additional work at home. Often, less competent teachers are assigned to easier courses and more motivated students. The administration justifies this by claiming that exceptional teachers work "better with the more difficult students." Such inequities are grossly unfair especially when taken in conjunction with salary scales that are identical for teachers regardless of quality or effort. Teachers are almost always paid on a salary scale which reflects the teacher's years of teaching experience coupled with academic credentials, so an ineffective teacher receives the same salary as an excellent one.

Another interruption in instruction is the test-driven curriculum, in which the presentation of prescribed content matter is suspended and replaced with teaching of a different variety, a procedure which many refer to as "teaching to the test."

Many jurisdictions have initiated competency or functional tests to ensure that a typical high school graduate has attained a basic level of ability in areas such as reading, writing, math and citizenship. The state of Maryland requires all students to pass a battery of functional skills. Despite the admirable premise that all students should actually be "educated" before receiving a diploma, these tests, and subsequent remediation for those who fail the tests, consume many hours for the teachers, as well as administrators and counselors, who are frequently needed to proctor the exams. Because of strict guidelines concerning proper administration of tests, an entire school can see its educational program disrupted for two or three days in a row for the testing of just one grade level. Classroom assignments for those not involved in the testing must be altered, causing confusion and general upset. If, for example, the ninth and eleventh graders are being tested, and the schedule is disturbed, the remaining seniors and sophomores may be shown a movie or not required to attend school at all on testing days.

Some blame bureaucrats who care more about the scores received than the actual quality of knowledge accumulated over four years. An extremely time-consuming undertaking, competency testing usually begins in the ninth grade with those who fail undergoing remediation and continual re-testing in each consecutive year until they eventually pass. Students are drilled in class or individually pulled from academic classes as they repeatedly complete exercises provided solely to prepare them to excel on standardized tests. Practice exams are administered to provide familiarity with the testing instrument. Instead of learning new material, students are taught how to take tests. The quality of instruction in the actual subject area frequently declines as teachers spend time coaching students to do well on the scheduled test. A social studies teacher explained, "I was constantly looking at what I was teaching with an eye to whether I was moving toward preparing the students for the functional test."

Extracurricular activities, ever-present in today's schools, also fill much of this unscheduled time, as the teacher-coach or sponsor formulates plans or attends to details totally unrelated to their subject matter. A sponsor whose class was responsible for raising approximately $10,000 to finance a prom said that dealing with fund-raisers and financial records alone was all-consuming. Added duties associated with the sales of candy or t-shirts included advertising, inventory, ordering, and distribution. He said, "I feel like I am not teaching. I am running a small business."

All high schools boast yearbooks, with the production of such a publication costing up to $30,000 annually. Funding must be acquired through sales and fund-raisers like dances, car washes, or innumerable other get-rich-quick schemes. Similarly, high school newspapers can cost more than $1,000 per issue to publish. The teacher in charge of these endeavors also must mastermind the acquisition of capital to keep these ventures afloat. Those in private business realize the effort that goes into procuring such sums of money. What would constitute a full-time job for others is a routine part of the day for the teacher who must take on these duties along with the primary responsibility of teaching five courses a day.

Good coaching, no matter what the sport, does not happen spontaneously either. A science teacher related, "To run a good practice and prepare students for a game, I must prepare much like I do for a chemistry class. If I am planning plays or drills, handling physical forms or counting uniforms, I do not have time to develop lessons." Yet teachers are expected not only to maintain, but also promote such programs by recruiting players, training them and also monitoring their academic performance despite the encroachment on their own preparation time. Another coach elaborated on the duties of the job which encompasses scheduling sports events, maintaining rosters, checking eligibility lists, and even arranging transportation for sports events. The most discouraging aspect of the coaching job for him was the necessity of personally arranging for fellow faculty members to cover classes he would miss while he was coaching. The combined inconvenience of creating extra lesson plans and relying on the good-heartedness of his busy colleagues to fill in for him not only infringed on his own class time, it burdened other non-coaching professionals as well, leading him to comment, "It is just one more expectation of the school hierarchy which does very little to help the teacher. The coach is expected to do extra and then has to suffer for it."

As non-teaching responsibilities grow each year, many educators are actively seeking new careers outside of the school, ready to leave a vocation they once loved, disappointed and disillusioned. Teachers surveyed by the Department of Education in 1987 indicated that 52 percent had seriously considered leaving teaching. More recent studies continue to show that teacher morale has declined with almost one third saying they would not choose to become teachers if they had it to do again. There are many rewards in a teaching career, but the job is getting progressively more difficult. "The teaching profession is under great strain," said a teacher from the state of Washington. "We're expected not only to teach but to help with the total ills of society. Student apathy has grown. . . . [there is a] loss of desire to be involved. We're overworked. . . . In short, we're burning out."

Chapter
Five

Who Teaches
The Teachers?

"The ideal classroom does not exist. I had an idealistic view of education, of teaching, but I found out very quickly that it was a lot more than I had ever expected and I was not at all prepared for that."

BETH WEITZ
STUDENT TEACHER

EVERY YEAR A NEW CROP OF IDEALISTIC, optimistic, and enthusiastic student teachers enters the public schools to undergo the practicum experience required to become certified teachers, only to have their naive expectations shattered as they discover that they are not adequately prepared to do the job. Fresh from the isolated confines of the university, having completed all of the required education courses, novice teachers are brimming with knowledge of their subject areas, philosophical theories of education, and creative lessons with which they truly expect to change the world. Unfortunately, the lack of practical techniques and basic classroom management skills renders them virtually helpless as they attempt to instruct actual students during their student teaching experience.

After they are finally hired to teach in the public schools, these newcomers face a different kind of challenge as they are abandoned during the grueling, solitary first year. Essentially thrown to the wolves, they must acclimate themselves with little backing or guidance from veteran teachers, school administrators or other school system personnel. Even the career teacher faces a constantly changing classroom atmosphere in which new techniques, subject matter, and teaching strategies are needed to facilitate learning. They, too, are left alone in a profession which illogically expects each individual to independently discover what truly works, without providing the effective training and professional enrichment so badly needed to revitalize sagging morales and maintain up-to-date instruction.

Other professionals in challenging positions work in a similar manner. "Rookies" are left to stumble through their initial year, learning as they go. If the young salesman needs to acquire more confidence or a better presentation, the company he works for may experience lower sales figures for a time only to recoup losses as the beginner polishes his performance. Inexperience is the norm for those launching a career immediately after college graduation. The ramifications of inexperience, however, are extremely serious in the public school classroom. Young teachers will learn and grow, but their students will never be able to reclaim the period of time they served as "guinea pigs" in a trial and error situation. The consequences are long-lasting and need not result if new teachers were better trained in universities and then nurtured during the first crucial year on the job.

Teacher training is sadly inadequate at the college level, almost totally absent during the first years of teaching, and grossly deficient as the professional progresses in a career. The most distressing lack of pertinent training for high school teachers comes at the university level.

Without exception, college education students speak of entering the teaching profession with hopeful idealism. Knowing that they will garner neither great professional status nor grandiose salaries, these individuals are motivated to teach for a wide variety of reasons. Some are vague about what leads them to the career, claiming that they had always wanted to teach and knew from the time they were children that this was the job for them. Others claim they really want to do something meaningful with their lives and help young people. A love of subject matter, coupled with the desire to share that subject, spurred still others. Some came from families of teachers and saw a life of teaching as the logical progression for themselves as well. Regardless of the reasons, prospective teachers enter college desiring to learn how to be effective in the classroom. Too often, they are bitterly disappointed with their university professors who subordinate practical teaching methods to esoteric theories and philosophical issues that bear little resemblance to the daily realities of the classroom. Most education students never observe a typical classroom or teach high school students until the third, or even fourth, year of college. Thus, they approach their final student teaching practicum with little idea of how actually to teach a class, or an understanding of what makes a truly effective teacher.

The lack of preparation for the real world of public school teaching is directly attributable to the lack of attention paid to the real mechanics of teaching by today's university schools of education. Lynne Cheney, chairman of the National Endowment for the Humanities, writes in *Tyrannical Machines,* "We force prospective schoolteachers to take education courses that waste their time." She adds, ". . . [these unfocused courses] . . . are more likely to confuse and mislead than to enlighten." Many times the sophisticated and theoretical concepts taught at the university are not even practiced at the high school level by working educators and student teachers are left feeling that their entire preparation in college was irrelevant. According to William D. Hawley, director for the center of educational policy at Vanderbilt University, this "discontinuity" between the university and the actual classroom is quite alarming.

Discrepancies between the skills new teachers need and want and the training they actually receive are disturbing, as education departments almost seem determined to prepare the new teacher for failure. They send the student teacher into the classroom defenseless, unarmed with the tools of the trade. Instead, they are crammed with obscure ideology that will barely help them get through a single class period. John I. Goodlad, professor of education and director of the Center for Educational Renewal at the University of Washington, examined teacher training programs in an extensive five-year study. Goodlad writes in *Teachers For Our Nation's Schools,* "Prospective teachers want to learn how to teach; they are not aspiring to be educational historians, philosophers, psychologists, or sociologists. Many of the professors of education they encounter early on, however, are precisely such specialists." Goodlad found that teacher candidates were unhappy that the foundations courses did not adequately guide them in teaching. Likewise, the study revealed, "Most had great difficulty recalling the substance of their foundations courses. Very little of what was discussed in an introductory course reappeared later for these students. They made no connection, it appeared, between the early discussion—or, to be more accurate, lectures—and their own teaching."

The need on the part of teacher candidates for practical techniques for functioning in the classroom is not surprising, as the school is the final and definitive testing ground for the teacher. Not being able to function effectively in the classroom is the nightmare of the teacher and the need for better pedagogical preparation is desperate. Due to a lack of proper training in the actual skills of instruction and management, teachers often flounder and fail in student teaching as well as during the first year on the job. The feeling of ineffectiveness and isolation is not unique to the first experience in any demanding job, but while the student teacher may get a $C-$ or a poor evaluation, it is the student who fails to learn geometry or biology.

The student teaching experience is often a lonely and eye-opening experience from which, after overcoming the initial shock, college students still emerge ready to commence a career in education. Zhixin Su writes in *Teachers For Our Nation's Schools,* "The organization of the training program, especially the structure of the student teaching experience . . . tends to encourage the development of teacher individualism. The image of student teachers projected in the present study is an aggregate of persons learning to teach on their own motivation and initiatives. The student teachers confront a 'sink-or-swim' situation in physical isolation. The way most beginners are inducted into teaching therefore leaves them doubly alone." Many never enter the profession because, unprepared for what they encounter, they suddenly experience so many harsh realities that teaching fails to be a desirable option for them. Beth Weitz, a young woman who developed a remarkable rapport with her students during her brief nine weeks of student teaching, said, "I don't think I am going to go right into teaching after college. The one thing I realized is that you have to be prepared to put your students, put the school, put everything in front of you. You have to sacrifice yourself for everyone else. To be perfectly honest, at the age of 22, I'm not sure I am ready to do that." With better university preparation for what really exists in a public high school, most student teachers could successfully complete training periods, and become valuable members of a profession badly in need of an infusion of enthusiastic professionals.

Prospective teachers often lack knowledge of teaching methods and classroom management techniques, as well as a sense of the personalities and problems of the high school students they are going to teach. Sadly, many colleges of education are cutting down on the number of practical courses that could provide this immediate knowledge, rather than expanding as the need expands. Jessie Bachike, after completing her student teaching, said, "Education classes in college equip you to deal with the ideal classroom that does not exist . . . one of our professors talked a lot about coming up with really creative lessons, but we never talked about how to deal with day-to-day teaching. I don't think I was prepared for the management problems either."

One student teacher admitted that her teaching methods course was more helpful than most education courses, but, "My biggest criticism was that we didn't have many secondary student teachers like me in the class, so the methods were geared toward elementary teachers." Preparation like this left the young woman frustrated and confused as she tried to adapt totally inappropriate techniques of instruction to a group of high school students.

It is not surprising that many young people are caught off guard by what they find as they enter the classroom as a teacher for the first time. Many have had little, or no, actual teaching experience before beginning student teaching, an experience which should serve as the culmination of a college career in educational training, not as a sort of "baptism-by-fire" initiation rite to test their mettle. Jeanne Lowrie, a talented and enthusiastic new teacher, said, "Prior to this student teaching experience, I had no experience in the classroom. We did little micro-teaching lessons where they brought in students and we taught for five minutes. That's not realistic. When you get to the real classroom, it's do or die."

Another student teacher told of a ridiculously contrived classroom setting arranged by the education department in which she was supposed to be able to practice teaching. "The high school kids came from some of the best private schools in the area. They were angels; they weren't like real kids. There were usually five students and they were surrounded by 18 college students, so of course they were not going to get out of line. They were your perfect class and they knew why they were there. They all put their hands up and tried to answer the questions." Any teacher knows that this scenario is never repeated in an actual classroom. To imply to teacher trainees that if they can teach in a rarified atmosphere such as the model classroom, then they will be competent on the job, is a gross miscarriage of trust.

These antiseptic, safe university experiences have little in common with actual high school classrooms, as the student teachers quickly discovered. "I just wasn't prepared for kid's who didn't do work and didn't care about their grades and acted as badly as they do," said Jessie Bachike. "The thing I find hardest is that there is no respect from the students. Then I go home and all I do is plan and mark papers. I get four hours of sleep and then come to school the next day and it just doesn't seem like I have any time to myself." Even though student teachers are often just four years removed from their own high school years, they have little experience to draw on. The aspects of teaching that a high school student actually observes are only a minute part of the complexities that must be dealt with every day by the teacher. Methods of preparation, discipline, and delivery of instruction are taken for granted and never analyzed by the high school student, while the scope and diversity of the teacher's duties remain hidden as well.

Ann Drew, now a full-time English teacher, related, "College had not prepared me to teach. I knew my stuff as a student, and performed well, but that wasn't much help when I was the teacher. I can look back now on student teaching and see how I was constantly being tested. When you come out of college and into the classroom to teach, you realize that being a student is a passive thing. Being on the flip side as the teacher, you realize how active an endeavor it is and completely different from performing well as a student. There were so many things that I had never formally been taught before that I was expected to know and do."

Even though the population entering the high schools exhibits more diverse needs, teachers are still being prepared as they were 40 years ago to teach a type of student that rarely, if ever, exists in a classroom atmosphere that in no way resembles past learning situations. Kenneth L. Peatross, executive director of the Minnesota Board of Teaching, said in

Education Week, "There's a lot of tension about the fact that teacher preparation is not in tune with practice, that, somehow, preparation is not keeping abreast of the advances that are being made in teaching and learning; that veteran teachers are out there floundering around and learning on the job; and that teacher education is blithely going along preparing people for 1950." Not only are teaching practices being omitted from college curriculum, the element that enables any learning at all to take place—effective classroom management—is rarely dealt with at all on the college level.

Discipline and behavior management are the areas in which student teachers are most ill-equipped to deal effectively. Fred H. Jones, in *Positive Classroom Discipline,* writes, "Any classroom has the potential of being a 'problem classroom.' The way in which discipline is managed in the classroom will govern to a large extent the amount of time that is spent working and the amount of time that is spent 'goofing off.' In dealing with the wide range of squirrelly behaviors that may come from a room full of young bodies, a skilled teacher needs a *wide range of management techniques.*

"Avoiding the topic of classroom discipline as though it were a taboo is nowhere more evident than in teacher education. It is a sobering exercise to look through the catalogs of teacher training programs at colleges and universities in an attempt to find a course entitled 'Discipline.' It is even more sobering to speak with teachers in the field about what teacher training they received concerning the management of classroom discipline. The responses are most commonly accompanied by either laughter or anger. The . . . most common replies are, 'The subject was never brought up' . . . or 'They told us we would pick it up on the job.' "

The abrogation of responsibility on the part of the college of education may serve as a pathetic admission that they do not, in fact, possess the expertise to instruct teacher candidates properly or fail to recognize the importance of such procedures. "The notion that teachers will somehow, magically, spontaneously learn how to keep thirty kids from going thirty different directions once the teachers are 'on the job' is amazing—a cruel hoax used to cover up a major deficiency in teacher training," concludes Jones.

One teacher from Iowa said, "Kids treated me badly. The options for discipline I didn't know. How does a student teacher or a new teacher know when it is all right to send a kid out of class and when it is not?" This knowledge cannot be gleaned intuitively, as many education schools seem to assume. Very real and teachable skills exist for the management of daily classroom situations, but they are not routinely taught at the university. Although they do not formally teach classroom procedure, some schools make the attempt to provide prospective teachers with a pedagogical background by placing them temporarily in schools in various capacities. However, the presence of a teacher trainee in a classroom does not automatically ensure that knowledge will be gained.

In an attempt to provide experience for the neophyte teacher, some universities require courses which predominantly consist of observation of high school teachers. In these courses, a student sits in on a class, observes the daily activities and interactions, then records observations to be submitted to their education professor for a grade. Unfortunately, these potentially advantageous exercises are negated by the lack of processing or analysis of the phenomena observed. At times such experiences can actually be harmful since the student teacher frequently has no idea of what caused certain behavior to occur, or what appropriate follow-up there might be after the trainee has left the class. The observer becomes competent in recording data in a prescribed form, but at best can come away from the experience with little new understanding of teacher-student interaction and, at worst, a misconception of classroom dynamics. Courses like this may actually be useless, according to Sharon Feiman-Nemser, in a report for The Institute for Research on Teaching at Michigan State University. She writes, "From more than 10,000 hours of exposure to teachers, prospective teachers have stored up countless impressions of life in the classroom. Because 'psyching out the teacher' may be crucial to a student's survival, it is often undertaken with considerable intensity. From this 'apprenticeship of observation,' students internalize models of teaching that are activated when they become teachers." With little or no understanding of the import of the actions, these models may be re-enacted, when the prospective teacher engages in field work.

To provide students with such an experience is an attempt to facilitate methodology, but is not effective unless the teacher being observed is an active part in the process. Most times, the teacher is left out of the process completely. One student teacher told of a situation in which she had real questions about what had transpired between student and teacher during her observation period. She left the school confused, however, because she felt too intimidated by the teacher to make any inquiry about the rationalization behind her methods. She also said, "I was not told that I should talk to her and I didn't want to inconvenience her. After all, she was busy." The university had structured the practicum so that the student entered the classroom after the teacher had begun her lesson and left before she was done, so there was no frame of reference for the lesson being taught. In fact, the student teacher had never seen the lesson presented so she had little idea of the implications of what had actually transpired.

Carleen Fritz, a dynamic young teacher said, "I learned through substitute teaching exactly how kids acted towards teachers, and even though I had been a sub and not the real teacher, kids' attitudes were more familiar to me. I heard the kids talking and learned what was important to them and it really opened my eyes to what schools and students were all about."

Even though she had prior classroom experience with a solid background in English, Fritz admitted that she never was taught how actually to teach a novel, a short story, or a poem in the four years she spent preparing to be a teacher. The required educational methods classes were useless to her when she began a student teaching assignment where she was asked to teach poetry, speech, and journalism. She said, "A student teacher is forced to take a methods course in sign language when you are going into English, and it costs $900 or $1,000. I could have really used that educational money somewhere else for something I really could have used, maybe taken another lit course, or a writing course, or even a speech course, something I would eventually teach. At this point I can still remember how to sign Whitney Houston's 'Greatest Love'. What good does that do me in teaching high school English?" Lynne Cheney writes in *Tyrannical Machine,* ". . . the time spent in these courses is time that cannot be spent studying history or mathematics, physics or French— the subjects that the teachers teach."

The consensus of most teachers about where they learned the most about actual teaching is unanimous—from the high school teachers they worked with, either during student teaching or during their first year on the job. According to an article by Lynn Olson in *Education Week,* "There should be more of a continuum between a teacher's pre-service and in-service training, and that many things now learned on campus would be better learned on the job. Most teachers complain that they never got enough instruction in classroom management before they began teaching . . . but studies have found that such lessons may be best learned after someone has already spent time in the classroom." The facilitation of in-school programs from the freshman year and throughout the training for an education career would provide the teacher trainee with the hands-on experience that would render them ready to function effectively in the classroom when it is time to student teach. The effectiveness of these in-school programs depends wholly on the quality of instruction given. Many times, college professors are not able to provide information needed because, in many cases, the education professors have never taught in a public school classroom. In cases like this, the students are being indoctrinated with the theory, "Do as I say, not as I do."

Despite assertions on the part of most new teachers that they really learned how to teach from the cooperating teacher in the high school, educators are largely ignored as a resource in-teacher training programs. A supervisor of student teachers from a large eastern university explained that there is an arrogant, elitist attitude among college professors concerning their secondary counterparts, "Schools of education do not bring in high school teachers, however, partly because they are the authorities and it is threatening to them and also because they really believe there is a difference between being a teacher and being a college professor."

Enlisting the expertise of high school teachers in the teacher training process is the easiest and most sensible remedy to the problem of teacher readiness—a solution largely avoided by the universities. The same supervisor explained, "Education schools could have people who are intimately involved in the high schools themselves, high school teachers. The most helpful and obvious resource for ed schools would be the teachers working in the schools in their districts. High school teachers are the most obvious and available experts in the area of education."

Yet high school teachers are ignored as a source of valuable, practical and up-to-date information about what is really happening in the classrooms. Instead, prospective teachers are herded into "Mickey Mouse" courses that do little for them.

In the student teaching experience, the most influential indicator of a student's potential in the profession, high school teachers are scorned as a resource. Many times, classroom teachers are selected to train a student teacher by arbitrary methods. No screening process is applied to determine who would be a proper mentor for the student and sometimes a teacher is assigned merely because it is his turn to have a student teacher. Incidents have even occurred where a teacher who refused to accept a trainee in the classroom was assigned under protest. The personal partnership between the student teacher and the cooperating teacher can mean certain success, or miserable failure if the two are mismatched. Teachers often have little or no warning that a student teacher will be working with them and, likewise, the student may find out just a few days before beginning their assignment where and what courses they will be teaching. With only a few days to prepare, the student teacher is often unfairly burdened with extensive planning to be hastily done, often without time to consult with the cooperating teacher. During the school day, little time exists for the mentor and trainee to confer as one is always either teaching or observing, so the student teacher is left to bear the brunt of going it alone.

Carleen Fritz, a teacher from New Jersey, felt she was more prepared than most during her student teaching experience, but attributed this mostly to her own initiative and pure luck. "I was lucky in the fact that I had substitute taught during college and in that sense had been around high school students more than the average student teacher. That's not to say you can master teaching just by substituting, but it gave me an advantage. That helped because if I hadn't done that, it would have been a real shocker to see what really went on in the public schools. You go in with this idealistic idea that all kids are going to do their schoolwork and that they want to learn and that is all shot down the first day.

A supervisor of student teachers from a prestigious eastern university explained the main problem in training teachers. "There is a great discrepancy between ivory tower theorizing and practical teaching and there is an important need for both of them, but most education schools do not have the resources or the time or priority of preparing students in a more practical way." John I. Goodlad, in a recent comprehensive study of teacher education, described such programs as being victims of "chronic prestige deprivation."

Ironically, even the supervisor of student teachers, the one university official who has the most influence in the teaching practicum, commands little respect or importance in the pre-

paratory stages. According to one supervisor, "Most of the
education departments work by having the education courses
taught by education faculty members and the field work, supervising the student teachers, done by someone who is familiar with teaching and the subject areas being taught. Universities relegate the supervising of student teachers to 'hired
guns' because it is a very low status position on the college
campus. To the student teachers, however, it is a very important position."

Adequate preparation will help produce confident, competent student teachers, but the nurturing of the teacher must
not stop at the undergraduate level. The first few years of
teaching, and particularly the first year, are more difficult in
many ways than the initial student teaching situation, largely
because the new teacher does it all alone. The number of
potentially excellent career educators lost to public schools
early in their professional experience could be reduced drastically if support were available for the rookie.

"Because of rising school populations and the high percentage of the nation's 2.5 to 3 million school teachers who are
nearing retirement, the United States will need to hire 1.5 to
2 million new teachers by 1997," reported Eric Goodman in
McCall's magazine, September 1990. The need for teachers is
clear, and schools must seek not only to attract new teachers,
they must protect and nurture those beginning their service
so they are teaching effectively now and in the future.

Lack of confidence on the part of the first-year teacher can
lead them to struggle unnecessarily because they dread revealing professional weakness. One new teacher, experiencing
difficulty with discipline, agonized for months over who to
turn to for help for fear of appearing to be the "weak link" in
the department. When she eventually confided in a fellow
teacher, she found that her situation was not unique, as many
rookies suffered from similar problems as they slowly gained
experience. When an experienced colleague made herself
readily available to discuss obstacles, the young teacher's con-

fidence and instructional skill both improved greatly. Had this beginner been assigned an official mentor from day one of her new career, countless hours of worry and frustration could have been eliminated.

A rookie teacher described the feelings of a first-year teacher, "The most frightening thing about teaching, especially being a new teacher, is that you are thrown into a room and expected to know what you are doing and there is nobody to give you any support. You are alone in the classroom with very little experience. If you have a problem, you have to completely reconstruct any given moment to a fellow teacher, because only a fellow teacher would care or understand it, but it is incredibly important to you to find out from someone else if you handled the moment properly, whether it is a disciplinary problem or a teaching method.

"I am the type who likes to over-prepare, but since I had no sense of my audience after only one semester of student teaching experience (in rural Iowa), I really didn't know what these kids were about. Suddenly I was the full-time teacher and I had no idea what was going to interest them or what would be above or below their level of ability. I didn't know how to package the material I had to teach to make it appealing, so there was a lot of wasted effort working extremely hard on the wrong things."

For some, the shock of isolation in a high school causes them to leave the profession. If help were more readily available, the 26 percent reported by the Carnegie Foundation as likely to leave the teaching profession in the next five years might remain in education. Teachers who are given support and training on the job do not leave the profession, they stay to mature and grow as experts in their areas. The morale of educators who feel valued because they are offered support do not become that 38 percent who said they were seriously considering leaving the teaching profession.

Mentoring programs for new teachers can alleviate much of the feeling of insecurity and isolation during the first year in the profession. One teacher had the good fortune to enter a school at mid-year and was able to observe and team teach for five weeks before picking up her own solo schedule. She remembered, "It was great. I was able to see *different* management techniques, different teacher temperaments and how kids reacted to different approaches and philosophies. I had a good bit of time to discuss different ideas with the teachers I had observed. When you come out of college you have had a practicum, in some cases, and a student teaching experience, but still that is only really one other teacher you have been exposed to before you have to develop you own teaching style. Everything else is relying on your memory to remember what teachers you had and how they taught you, who was good and who was bad and why. The opportunity to be with colleagues to brainstorm with, to commiserate with, to share the work load, to split up certain trouble kids was invaluable."

Clearly, all school systems could benefit from the professional enrichment of all faculty members. Even the seasoned veteran needs time for professional interaction and additional training in new methodology and practices. Gary Sykes, in *Restructuring Schools,* writes, "If teaching is equated solely with student contact and consequently with isolation from other adults, teachers will have few opportunities to improve their practices or to develop professional orientations and commitments. To implement the other principles, teachers must have time to plan, to confer, to observe teaching by other teachers, to discuss practice, to read and write, to travel, and to reflect and inquire. Finding or creating time is the central imperative in the management of teaching."

Sykes points out that, ". . . teachers work alone and receive little feedback. Many teachers neither observe teaching nor have their teaching observed by colleagues. Schedules preclude much collaborative planning. Funds are unavailable for work in the summers. Teachers have little access to sabbaticals, to conferences and workshops, to good university courses. Districts vary in their resource commitments to staff development, but most offer two to three days of teacher training per year and tie up most of their teacher-development budget in salary increases for desultory course taking and empty credentialism at local universities. So professionalism conceived as commitment to reflection and inquiry into teaching, continuous growth of knowledge and skill, receives little material or organizational support in most schools."

Training that is provided for teachers often stems from poorly conceived ideas of what the educational bureaucracy thinks teachers need. These ideas are packaged as tedious and unproductive presentations that leave teachers wishing they had just been allowed time to grade papers or plan for the next day.

Many school districts provide a form of training to their teachers which is ineffective at best, and extremely distasteful at worst. Through inservice classes and workshops, training is provided and often required, but too often the information dispersed through these avenues as a response to one of the latest educational trends or politically popular concepts. Rarely do they give the teachers what they really need—practical solutions and lessons that can be taken immediately back to the classroom and actually used. Often in-service courses are not aimed at the enrichment of teachers, but are merely held to satisfy school district requirements or contractual obligations. School systems institute these programs to inculcate faculty in new management systems or new curriculum with training that is perfunctory and often poorly presented. The feeling of all involved is sometimes, "We have to do this, so let's just get it over with." Little follow up ensues, so teachers file the newly presented information away, never to be used again, and heave resigned sighs at yet another large block of wasted time.

Lynne Cheney, in *Tyrannical Machines,* writes "Teachers are commonly expected to participate in some kind of continuing education, but the 'in-service' courses their schools and school districts offer seldom provide the valuable experience (they need). Typical in-service classes in Baltimore, Maryland, are 'Interaction: Human Concerns in the Schools' and 'Creative Teaching Strategies.' A recent report noted that grades are not given in the Baltimore classes and that few, if any, texts or papers are assigned. In Fairfax County, Virginia, teachers were recently encouraged to take in-service training in which they studied such topics as 'withitness' and 'subparameters of momentum.' A North Carolina educator reports that teachers in the Charlotte-Mecklenburg school district study the twenty-eight characteristics of 'effective teaching'— which they are then expected to demonstrate in each lesson. Small wonder that across the nation, teachers use the phrase *in-service* in the passive ('we were in-serviced')—as though something rude and unpleasant had been done to them."

Once again, however, experts in the field of teaching, actual successful classroom teachers, are largely ignored in the area of in-service training. One parent, noting an exceptionally good high school teacher, wondered why that teacher could not train colleagues in successful methods for the classroom. She said, "Teachers who are very successful should teach in-service for colleagues at their school. That is what cooperation is all about. A teacher who identifies successful strategies should be sharing them with other teachers." Clearly, a teacher at a given school has a better sense of what is needed for others at the same school to teach effectively, as all schools differ in the needs of the students and community.

Well-trained teachers produce well-educated students. Even though problems exist to challenge a teacher's effectiveness in the classroom, a prepared professional can deal with them adeptly. Teachers who are provided, both in college and during their careers, with the vital techniques with which to control classroom environment gain the ability to effectively teach what needs to be taught. The direct outcome of support being readily available is a better educational situation for both students and teachers.

Chapter
Six

The Formidable

Teacher Unions

"The Achilles heel of the teaching profession is that it treats
everyone, good or bad, as interchangeable."

CHESTER E. FINN

TWO MAJOR TEACHER UNIONS, the National Education Association (NEA) and the American Federation of Teachers (AFT),
have been primarily responsible for creating and shaping the
current system of public education in the United States. With
a combined membership of almost three million teachers,
these organizations represent a formidable and potent force
in both American society and politics. They regularly negoti-
ate local salary contracts for teachers, dictate certification requirements for prospective educators and increasingly engage
in partisan political activities. Yet ironically, these unions,
which profess to have the best interest of America's teachers
and school children at heart, have also become major obstacles
to substantive educational reform. Virtually every major educational problem facing the public schools is simplistically
reduced to a matter that somehow can be miraculously solved
by improved teacher pay and additional government appropriations. In the past decade, the fallacy of such arguments
have become painfully apparent. Teacher salaries increased

steadily during the eighties, to a respectable nationwide average of $33,015. In Alaska, Connecticut, New York, and Washington, D.C., the median income for educators is in excess of $40,000. Cost-per-pupil spending likewise increased 33 percent in *real* dollars. Despite this unprecedented taxpayer commitment, American high school students as a whole still fail to meet even minimal expectations.

The current American educational system, with its strong national unions and state funded public schools, is a relatively recent development. During the early colonial period, education, except in New England, was seen as strictly a private matter with little government interest, intervention, or involvement. In the rural South, the lack of established towns coupled with the great distances between farms and plantations conspired to prevent any realistic form of centralized schooling. Instead, the more prosperous planters preferred to send their children back to England for their formal education. The vast majority, though, could provide only some rudimentary instruction at home, with simple lessons usually taught by family members. Still others who could afford the expense, hired private male tutors to live on their estates. These early teachers quickly became valued and cherished members of the family and taught daily in a small room specially set aside for classes, with children from neighboring farms often in attendance. Colonial students, though, were schooled only in reading, elementary arithmetic, and other basic skills deemed crucial for eventually establishing and running their own plantations.

Throughout the South, there was powerful resistance to any form of government-sponsored, free, public schools. Governor William Berkeley of Virginia, for instance, wrote in the 17th century, "I thank God, there are no free schools nor printing, and I hope we shall not have these [for a] hundred years; for learning has brought disobedience, and heresy, and sects into the world, & printing has divulged them, and libels against the best government. God keep us from both."

By contrast, the New England colonies were far more interested in establishing a uniform system of public education. Motivated primarily by a strong communal desire that their children learn to read in order to study the lessons of the Bible, some towns passed local ordinances as early as 1647 to levy public taxes for the support of small schools. Despite these early efforts, it was conservatively estimated that on the eve of the American Revolution, over 50 percent of men and 75 percent of women in America were virtually illiterate.

The establishment of a new American republic in 1776 gave impetus to the public school movement in the United States. Many of the founding fathers became strong proponents of state-run public schools, arguing that an educated and informed citizenry was vital to the preservation of liberty and the protection of individual rights. Thomas Jefferson was one of the first to call for public financing of local community schools throughout the United States. He wrote, "I have indeed two great measures at heart, without which no republic can maintain itself. 1. That of general education, to enable every man to judge for himself what will secure or endanger his freedom. 2. To divide every county into hundreds, of such size that all the children will be within reach of a central school in it."

Such persuasive appeals did little to speed progress toward a truly universal system of public education. Only as the nation's demographics changed and the country became more settled and densely populated, was Jefferson's dream partially realized. By 1830, though, many states in the East and Midwest, along with some local communities, had established the first secular, tax-supported one-room school houses. All students were grouped together regardless of age or ability and were severely disciplined for any rules infraction. They learned primarily through memorization and recitation, constantly reading passages from the morality-laden *McGuffey Readers* which emphasized such important character traits as honesty, thrift, and industry.

With the onset of the American Civil War in 1861, the nation's classrooms were virtually emptied of male teachers who patriotically answered the call to arms. Local communities scrambled to replace them with women instructors and were soon pleased to find them not only competent, dedicated, and qualified, but willing to work for considerably less pay. Teaching soon became perceived nationwide as a noble calling rather than a professional career with teachers expected to provide a sound moral example for their students and to abide by strict societal codes of behavior. A typical teacher contract from the turn of the century read:

Miss _____ agrees:

1. Not to get married. This contract becomes null and void immediately if the teacher marries.
2. Not to have company with men.
3. To be at home between the hours of 8:00 pm and 6:00 am unless in attendance at a school function.
4. Not to loiter downtown in ice cream stores.
5. Not to leave town at any time without the permission of the Chairman of the Trustees.
6. Not to smoke cigarettes. This contract becomes null and void immediately if the teacher is found smoking.
7. Not to drink beer, wine or whiskey. This contract becomes null and void immediately if the teacher is found drinking beer, wine or whiskey.
8. Not to ride in a carriage or automobile with any man except her brother or father.
9. Not to dress in bright colors.
10. Not to dye her hair.
11. To wear at least two petticoats.
12. Not to wear dresses more than two inches above the ankles.
13. To keep the schoolroom clean:
    (a) to sweep the classroom floor at least once daily.
    (b) to scrub the classroom floor at least once weekly with soap and hot water.
    (c) to clean the blackboard at least once daily.
    (d) to start the fire at 7:00 am so that the room will be warm at 8:00 am when the children arrive.
14. Not to wear face powder, mascara or to paint the lips.

According to Pamela Michael in an article in *Spectrum* magazine, "Although schoolteaching is one of the few professions into which women made early inroads, the fact that school boards demanded unmarried women as teachers necessarily made teaching something of a temporary job on the road to matrimony for many. As late as the 1930's, 77 percent of school districts employed no married women as new teachers and 62 percent required teachers to resign if they married. (Moviegoers in the 1930's saw nothing unusual about *Little Rascals'* teacher Miss Crabtree taking over for Miss Mc-Gillicuddy who has to resign in order to get married.) Before World War I, teachers in many small communities dared not go to the theater. Card playing and dancing were also forbidden. As late as 1929, a Kansas board of education fired eleven high school teachers for attending a local country club dance."

In an effort to improve the overall standards and quality of the evolving American educational system, the first teacher association was founded in 1857. Known initially as the National Teachers' Association, its name was later changed to the National Education Association. A noble charter promised to "elevate the character and advance the interests of the profession of teaching and to promote the cause of popular education in the United States." In 1916, a rival to the NEA was formed with the founding of the American Federation of Teachers in Chicago, Illinois. The AFT quickly became associated with the trade union movement then at its peak in the United States when it became affiliated with Samuel Gompers' American Federation of Labor.

During the Progressive period in the early 20th century, both unions worked diligently to improve the quality of the nation's rapidly growing teaching force. Certification standards were adopted in many states as a prerequisite for a teaching license and hundreds of "Normal Schools" or teaching colleges were established in an effort to formalize teacher training in order to better prepare educators for the modern, 20th century classroom. During this time, the educational philosophies of John Dewey were adopted by most educators, replacing archaic teaching methods with a new emphasis on humanizing instruction, accentuating the importance of the individual, and stressing the concept of learn-by-doing. In later years, both the NEA and AFT became early advocates of civil rights legislation, proponents of integration of the nation's classrooms, champions of equal educational opportunities, and vocal spokesmen for improved teacher contracts. They also conducted scholarly research on learning, and published important teaching aids, all of which greatly enhanced the quality of American education.

By the early sixties, the unions became increasingly militant in their demands for increased salaries, collective bargaining agreements, and larger government appropriations. These new priorities tended to subordinate other, more elusive educational issues and led the public to question for the first time the commitment of educators to their chosen profession. According to Brian Rowan, writing in *Restructuring Schools,* ". . . the militant assertion of teacher rights may have undercut esteem for teaching as a noble, helping profession."

Salaries and benefits became a source of perpetual contention between the unions and local governments. Teachers, represented by their unions, demanded large salary increases, arguing that better compensation would improve morale, redress past inequities, and attract better qualified people into the profession. But with employee salaries constituting up to 80 percent of the entire educational budget in most school districts, politicians balked at giving huge raises coupled with elaborate benefit packages, which would result in massive tax increases and discontent among other public employees such as police and firemen. The impasse led many local union chapters to resort to the traditional tool of organized labor to coerce compliance with their demands—the strike.

For the first time, many educators began to march in picket lines in an effort to close schools during their protest. In 1979 alone, there were over 350 teacher strikes nationwide. Unfortunately, these tactics often alienated the teachers' most logical allies, the parents and students. Many felt angry, frustrated, and victimized since they bore no personal responsibility for the salary disputes and yet they bore the brunt of the consequences of job actions. In one district in Pennsylvania, a typical teacher strike effectively closed the high schools for the first five weeks of the new year. Principals, administrators, and other substitutes, although vehemently denounced as "scabs" by the union, were desperately deployed to hold required classes for seniors so that the students could still apply to colleges, graduate on time, and make future plans. The classes that were held, however, only fulfilled the state requirement for minimum attendance, but did little to address the more important academic needs of the seniors. Once the strike was concluded and the teachers finally returned to the classroom, the remaining underclassmen were forced to endure extended hours and classes on Saturdays and holidays to make up for lost time. Such labor practices, although certainly effective, irreparably damage the general public's perception of teachers.

Strikes became an annual occurrence in many large metropolitan areas forcing some states to pass statutes prohibiting such walkouts by public employees. Faced with potentially crippling fines and court imposed injunctions, the unions in these jurisdictions devised other equally effective tactics to persuade local politicians to comply with union contract demands. The most common type of job action continues to be "work-to-the-rule" where union officials insist that its members honor only the specific duties required by their contract and do only a minimal amount of work. Papers go ungraded, homework unassigned, field trips cancelled, and student activities unchaperoned leaving the students disillusioned and powerless. Chester Finn, writes in his book, *We Must Take Charge,* "A revealing episode occurred on Long Island when school opened in September 1990. As reported in the *New York Times,* Laurette Holdridge, a brand-new second grade instructor, spent the first day getting acquainted with her students. She had devoted many hours of her own time during the summer to selecting library books for the children, had rehearsed the story she would read aloud to them during their first morning, had even memorized the questions she would ask them. The youngsters were charmed and, by day's end, had no desire to leave their wonderful new teacher. 'We don't want to go,' several cried. But rather than linger over another story, Miss Holdridge escorted them to the door promptly at 2:35 and exited the building herself five minutes later. The Mineola teachers, it turned out, had been without a new contract for some months, and as a result their union had declared a 'work-to-contract' job action. So much for eager second-graders. So much for professionalism."

Teachers are entitled to demand improved salary and benefits. Local school boards, even during austere economic times, likewise, must resist political pressures to undo the salary gains made during the eighties by balancing the budget at the expense of teachers and other civil servants and to offer a decent wage that will enable educators to live in the community they serve. But both the NEA and AFT have hurt legitimate salary aspirations by perpetrating the myth that by merely increasing funding for education and raising pay, all of the current problems faced by the schools will somehow be mysteriously solved. In fact, bad teachers will not suddenly become good teachers with additional pay and, with each union demand for more money, larger salaries, and additional programs, the already heavy tax burden imposed upon citizens in most localities is invariably increased.

Critics have rightly been suspicious of grandiose claims that more money automatically means better schools. On the contrary, Dr. Finn writes, ". . . in 1966 the United States Office of Education quietly published what would in time be seen as a blockbuster study by James S. Coleman and his associates. Its title was *Equality of Educational Opportunity.* . . . Among its many finds, however, was a profound challenge to the conventional wisdom: Coleman reported that student achievement did *not* vary from school to school in close relation to the resources present in those schools. The implication, of course, was that boosting school inputs did not reliably lead to stronger education outcomes, at least when the latter are defined in terms of pupil learning. The insight was portentous."

For generations, the nation's parochial schools have continually produced generations of well-prepared, competent students at substantially less cost than the public schools. Furthermore, if money alone were the answer, then the District of Columbia's public school system would logically be the nation's showcase. The city spends $7,407 annually to educate each individual student enrolled in the schools, the fourth highest expenditure in the entire nation. Teacher salaries *average* $42,288 and yet despite this enormous financial commitment to education, the dropout rate for the District's teenagers is an abominable 43 percent. The median student grade point average for all students is only a $D+$ while fully one-fourth of all grades assigned in the schools are Fs. Scott Shuger, the editor of the *Washington Monthly,* writes: "The average public school in the District has 45 fire code violations—and there have been attempts to remedy only half of them. The majority of D.C. school buildings have been poorly maintained for decades. Many classrooms are unheated; students and faculty have been injured by falling ceiling tiles, plaster, and window frames. Bathrooms with stopped-up toilets and sinks are commonplace. The showers in some locker rooms have not worked in 25 years. Some schools have only cold water; 24 have no running water at all. There are also chronic shortages of toilet paper, paper towels, and light bulbs. Some schools, apparently not getting any help from the General Supply Specialists, the Supply Management Office, or the Inventory Management Specialist downtown (each drawing a salary of $35,294) in their attempts to get soap, make their own."

The NEA and AFT have increasingly begun to look towards Washington and the federal government for the solution to their funding goals. Through skilled and intense political pressure, the unions convinced the Carter administration to create the Department of Education in 1979, separating the agency from its traditional place at Health, Education, and Welfare. The new cabinet agency helped focus the nation's attention on the problems faced by the public schools but the role of the federal government in education remains Constitutionally limited. The Department of Education's primary mission continues to lie in helping the disadvantaged, handicapped, or impaired student—populations whose unique needs may not be met adequately addressed by state and local governments. The public schools in general, though, are funded by a community's real estate and property taxes while the state legislatures and local school boards establish educational priorities. The union leadership apparently is oblivious to such facts and today are more at home lobbying in the hallowed corridors of Congress than in the reality-laden hallways of the public schools. Former Secretary of Education William Bennett commented, "All of the education groups—NEA, AFT, PTA—have big Washington offices. Their focus is here instead of where it should be. Washington can't make good schools or raise children."

Both unions have become more interested in being involved in national politics and advancing an ambitious, new social agenda rather than promoting legitimate educational goals. The annual NEA and AFT delegate assembly is representative of this new partisan mission. Each summer, representatives of local union chapters gather in a major metropolitan area ostensibly to draft regulations, adopt resolutions, and make proposals. The 8,000 teachers who attend the NEA assembly and the 2,300 delegates to the AFT convention, despite their numbers, still represent only a small fraction of teachers. Yet these delegate assemblies endorse political candidates and feel unconstrained in claiming to speak for the entire teaching profession.

The delegates honestly debate and take stands on valid educational issues such as homework, discipline, bilingual education, class size, and childhood education, but recent assemblies have strayed far beyond the limited realm of their expertise. For instance, the NEA convention in Miami in 1991 hurriedly adopted a statement expressing teachers' "grave concern" over the nomination of Judge Clarence Thomas to the United States Supreme Court. During the same convention after adopting a self-righteous resolution condemning censorship, pro-life delegates were hypocritically banned from wearing buttons and distributing literature supporting their viewpoint. Likewise, the Boy Scouts of America were expelled from an exhibition area. In an article for *Education Week,* Karen Diegmueller reported, "Blake Lewis, the national spokesman for the Scouts, said members of the [NEA's] gay and lesbian caucus had visited the booth on the previous day to tell the organization it should not be exhibiting there due to its ban on participation by homosexuals and girls and its requirement that members pledge an oath to God—positions that conflict with NEA anti-discrimination policies."

In previous years, similar delegate conventions have gone on record to oppose ozone pollution, to favor statehood for the District of Columbia, to advocate world peace, and to express their solemn belief "that Arbor Day should be observed each year in every state." NEA delegates voiced teachers' opposition to holding a PGA golf tournament in Alabama, urged members to boycott Folger's coffee, and encouraged protests against logging in the redwood forests of California. The AFT conference simultaneously demanded that the United States recognize the independence of Lithuania, extend health and insurance benefits to so-called "domestic partners," and endorsed a United Auto Workers boycott of Nissan, Honda, and Isuzu.

Most classroom teachers are uninvolved in their union's political stands. The adopted resolutions are not widely publicized among members and are printed in the professional journals in microscopic type. Jeff Dunson, a social studies teacher and a member of the NEA, commented after a recent convention, "Historically, when unions take on other political objectives beyond their expertise, they are doomed. Education is the number one issue in today's society. How many more issues do we have to deal with?"

Since 1976, the NEA has endorsed candidates in presidential elections. Beginning with Jimmy Carter, the union has supported the Democratic nominee in each subsequent campaign. The union's general membership has never been consulted or entrusted with such political decisions. One teacher remembered, "In 1988, several of us were sitting around the table having lunch when our local union president came in. After a few minutes of idle chat, he announced in cavalier fashion, 'We're going to endorse Michael Dukakis for president this week. His campaign people came to us and said that if we wanted NEA delegates to the Atlanta convention we had better go on record now.' It was incredible. No one ever asked any of us our opinions, it was a *fait accompli*." An interesting survey, recently completed by the Carnegie Institute, revealed that the union's endorsements may not accurately reflect the political philosophies of teachers. The study found that 42 percent of all teachers classified themselves as conservative while an additional 29 percent considered themselves to be moderate. Furthermore, exit poll data from the last three presidential elections indicated that teachers voted for the Republican candidate at roughly the same percentage as the general population.

When William Bennett was appointed by then President Ronald Reagan to serve as the new Secretary of Education, the union leadership attempted to flex its political muscle. Bennett recalled the first meeting he had with the NEA to discuss forthcoming educational policy: "The leadership of NEA . . . said let's try and work together because it will not be constructive for you not to work with us. I said, 'I translate that as we get along or you bust my knee caps.' Later, I went to Tucson to an elementary school and I was ambushed. The local union had arranged for several Hispanic children in third grade to stand up and ask me in English and Spanish why I was opposed to them speaking Spanish. Why did I hate Spanish? So the hardball was hardball, and it gives the profession a bad name and that's the way they behave."

In an effort to increase its power and influence on the national level, the NEA created its first political action committee, NEA-PAC, in 1972. Designed to solicit and collect voluntary contributions from its massive membership, the fund was empowered to appropriate up to $5,000 for candidates to national political office based ostensibly upon their commitment to advancing the union's educational and social agenda. Joe Standa, a Senior Professional Associate with the union, claimed that this development reflected the growing awareness among teachers that virtually all educational decisions were, in fact, political and that the "nonpartisan" NEA-PAC would increase the power of teachers in the shaping of the nation's educational policies. Most NEA chapters mirrored the example of the national headquarters with the creation of their own county and state PACs in an effort to sway local elections. The decision concerning who should receive these political funds and receive the union's political endorsement is never voted upon by the union's general membership or even its PAC contributors. Instead, special committees or delegate assemblies aristocratically decide such matters.

Since its inception, NEA-PAC has grown to become the third largest political war chest in the nation, surpassed only by the National Association of Realtors and the American Medical Association. When combined with the substantial contributions of a similar AFT political action committee, though, the teacher unions represent the largest single interest group in the United States. During the 1990 Congressional elections, alone, the NEA and AFT spent over $5.2 million in political contributions. That year, the national NEA endorsed 225 Democrats running for political office and 47 Republicans while the AFT supported 219 Democrats and 15 Republicans. In Maryland, where teacher unionism is relatively strong, 91 percent of all political endorsements in contested races were for the Democratic contender. The unions also deployed their substantial resources to support endorsed candidates with direct mail appeals, production of political commercials, and the printing of sample ballots indicating union endorsed candidates for distribution to its membership. In *We Must Take Charge,* Chester Finn writes, "The NEA and AFT are much the largest and most politically sophisticated of the establishment organizations, and they're active at local, state, and national levels. Their PACs are among the richest, right up there with the postal workers, the trial lawyers, and the bankers. Their bumper stickers, 'public-service' ads, columns, and press conferences are highly visible. The threat of a strike by one of their major locals is enough to bring many a community to its knees. Their political directors and lobbyists are among the smartest and toughest of any organization's. When an issue matters to them, they'll pull out all the stops. (The Oregon affiliate of the NEA devoted a million dollars in 1990 to defeating the state tuition tax credit initiative, a sum vastly greater than proponents had to spend.) They also involve themselves deeply in congressional and legislative races, sometimes running candidates from within their own ranks. When the AFT launched a 'Governor's Project' in July 1990, designed to 'shape the agenda' of thirty-six gubernatorial races later that year, and held out the promise of money and electoral help for candidates the union decided to endorse, we can fairly assume that those running for governor in 36 states took notice. We can also assume that many judged it would be in their interest to win the favor of the teacher unions. Some doubtless had already come to that conclusion."

Another area where the unions have had enormous influence has been in the evaluation and assessment of teachers and their classroom performance. After years of negotiations, the entire educational system is based upon the preposterous notion that all teachers are equally competent and hence interchangeable. There are no salary rewards or incentives to encourage excellence and little accountability to discourage ineptitude.

In the vast majority of school districts around the country, teachers are paid solely upon the basis of seniority. Each year, a teacher receives a union negotiated step increase often coupled with a cost-of-living adjustment (COLA). These pay raises are guaranteed regardless of a teacher's individual performance. Thus, a second-rate educator with more years of service receives greater salary compensation than an outstanding young teacher.

In a typical year, a tenured teacher is rarely observed by administrators more than twice. Most performance evaluations are announced in advance which allows even inferior teachers the opportunity to prepare a lesson plan that will disguise their incompetency. As a result, few teachers are ever dismissed for poor job performance. In any given school, there are those occasional teachers who do little preparation or anything to inspire and motivate their students. Nancy Adelman of Policy Studies Associates observed, "I've just seen too many instances in my travels of teachers working to the regulations of their contract and have the attitude I am out-of-here at 3:30. I come in here and I do this job from 8:30 to 3:30. They are punching a clock." These educators spend their days reading the newspaper, giving meaningless busy work to students, or showing endless hours of video tapes. One assistant principal observed, "We have been so quick with the unions to defend each other, we need to weed out among ourselves. Some teachers need to be gone. They are not good for kids. They are collecting checks and that's all and the kids know it. Some students come to me and say, 'He doesn't like kids.' They are in the wrong profession with that kind of attitude. You can have all of the subject matter [knowledge] in the world and be brilliant but if you don't have a love for kids, you're not going to be successful."

The unions, however, feel obligated to defend any of its members from charges of incompetency. This does prevent some unjust harassment and vindictive allegations against teachers and ensures a reasonable degree of due process, but it also protects many undeserving educators. Virtually every personnel matter will be litigated, with union-hired lawyers contesting even well-documented evidence of poor teacher performance and behavior. One California superintendent claimed that it costs between $100,000 and $400,000 for a school system to dismiss just one teacher. Thus, many jurisdictions simply allow the incompetent to continue with their contracts regardless of the educational harm they may impose upon students. An assistant principal in the Baltimore metropolitan area recounted an ongoing problem the school had with an alcoholic teacher who was continually drinking while in school. In frustration she confided, "A teacher almost must expose themselves or do something criminal to be fired. You can't fire a teacher today. We have a teacher with a 2-inch file but you can't bring up previous problems. You have to deal with each incident individually. There is no proving incompetency. This woman is a discredit to the profession and yet she is still there in the classroom! Other teachers even testified against her that she hit a kid. . . . I really resent the fact that the unions will not allow us to police our own profession. I respect the teaching profession and if I care for kids, certain teachers do not belong in class."

With the current ineffective teacher evaluation system firmly entrenched in the United States, school boards have attempted to lessen the adverse consequences of poor teachers by creating detailed and specific programs of studies in virtually all courses. The noble intent is to provide a certain level of basic competency in all classes regardless of the teacher. Detailed calendars, specific lessons plans, and extensive vocabulary lists are all provided in these centrally controlled curricula, but there are many adverse consequences inherent in this growing trend. Nancy Adelman observed, "Where the union is so strong, teachers don't seem to have a sense of themselves as professionals. Once you have that mentality, they create the teacher-proof curriculum where every little objective is laid out, there is a standard way of doing it, and every teacher will be on the same page at the same time." The opportunity for teachers to use innovation and creativity to help motivate students is often quite limited. Talented teachers are left feeling frustrated and angry while the students tend to lose the sense of vitality of a course. The end result is that everyone is brought down to a certain level of mediocrity, with excellence neither expected nor achieved.

The institutional protection of poor teachers has proven to be a persistent problem and does much to thwart the valid demands of educators that they be treated as skilled and competent professionals. Strikes, job actions, contract disputes, and blatant partisan political activities have likewise led to general public disfavor. With the problems of the public schools reaching near crisis proportions, both the NEA and the AFT have forsaken their traditional leadership role as educational reformers. Instead, they are now widely perceived as being part of the ever-increasing number of special interest groups who are determined to monopolize educational policy in the United States. The result has been the perpetuation of a system of public schools which continues to fail a large portion of its students.

Equal Education

for All

> "Knowledge will forever govern ignorance; and a people who mean to be their own governors must arm themselves with the power which knowledge gives."
>
> JAMES MADISON

THE DEMOCRATIC COMMITMENT OF THE United States to providing a quality education to all of its citizens remains the educational system's greatest strength. Unlike most other countries, all students are provided with many opportunities to obtain a high quality education. Unfortunately, many students still do not secure the vital knowledge and skills they need to succeed after graduation. While poor academic achievement permeates all levels of society, black and Hispanic students as a group continue to perform well below their schoolmates. Even though much is being done nationwide in a concerted effort to alleviate this serious problem, parents, students, teachers, and communities must reassess their roles in the educational process and take immediate action to correct the inequity of accomplishment that currently exists.

Despite the fact that most minority students attend the same schools, have the same teachers, and take the same classes as other students, the question that continues to perplex American educators is why all students do not achieve on roughly the same academic level. So far, the answers have been elusive despite countless reports, endless studies, and millions of dollars in expenditures. Repeatedly, the blame for such failure is consigned solely to the schools with critics charging that teachers are insensitive and dismissing the standard curricula as culturally biased. But public schools are not completely culpable for this deplorable situation. Deteriorating family conditions have been a major contributing factor as well as adverse peer pressure on students possessing low self-esteem. All combined, they lead students toward failing to take advantage of the many resources currently available to them in the public schools. Others simply reject education as "uncool" and ridicule their fellow classmates who do strive to achieve.

The pressing issue of low minority achievement is too often and too easily excused by politicians and school bureaucrats as a hopeless situation caused by poverty level, societal breakdown, and the very real problems of the inner-city. One concerned black mother, however, questioned such comfortable rationalizations claiming, "The syndrome we are talking about relative to the failure of minority students does not have anything to do with social or economic status. Everything I read has to do with the under privileged and the inner-city student, meaning poor. The phenomena that I see cuts across every line known to man. Kids who fail academically come from homes with two parents with lots of money who have an education far beyond just four years of college as well as kids with the single mother, aunt, or grandmother with very meager circumstances. There is no difference as far as their [children's] view of their own prospects."

Jawanza Kunjufu, president of African-American Images, attributes the widening academic gap between white and black students to five major factors: low teacher expectations, poor parental support, low student self-esteem, and an irrelevant curriculum taught with an inappropriate methodology for many African-American students. One of the most potent and destructive influences in the black community, according to Kunjufu, is the powerful but negative effect of the adolescent peer group. He writes in *To Be Popular or Smart: The Black Peer Group,* "It is very possible for parents to be supportive and teachers to have high expectations, and it all go for naught because the Black peer group is more concerned about what clothes you wear, how well you dance or play basketball, than academic achievement." He continues, "The phenomenon of peer pressure and its impact on achievement has reached a point that to do well academically is to act white and risk being called a nerd or a brainiac. For males, the peer pressure is so great, you may be called a sissy."

The stigma of being considered "too white" if they strive for academic excellence instead of activities like sports or music, is an all too real onus for many minority youths. Not only is this sneering attitude toward achievement demoralizing for the hard working student, it is destructive and demeaning when the inference is that scholastic success is incompatible with minority values. This pervasive attitude about academics is one that must be immediately challenged and changed.

Myla Kimbrough, an outstanding minority student and a recent graduate of Spellman College, remembers feeling like she did not fit in anywhere during her high school years. "I was ostracized from the black community in my high school because I was one of a handful of affluent, high-achieving blacks. There was that resentment from the blacks that were bussed out of their neighborhoods to go to a white school. To be re-segregated into the classrooms was something else. If you were not placed in remedial classes which were all black classrooms, then you were one of two or three blacks in all-white classes and that was intimidating." Not only did she feel out of place in such courses, black peers harassed her for betraying her peer group by trying to achieve. She explained, "Being in the higher level classes caused so much strife within my black peer groups because I was achieving. Some looked at me as if I was 'too white' because I was achieving. A black student who wants to talk articulately and use standard English is looked at as something unusual." For those students not willing or able to withstand such intense peer pressure, rebellion or resignation was the answer. Even for a student who seemed to fit in academically, the social sacrifices were great as Kimbrough readily admits, "I ended up having very few black friends in high school because I wanted to succeed. I just went to school and came home."

Drew Brown, the founder and president of the American Dream Program, chides students on perpetuating this perpetual cycle of failure. In a recent television interview Brown maintained, "There is no black or white, it is only ignorance and intelligence . . . this is simple. If you don't get an education you're not going to make it in this country." He sees the educational opportunities for minority youth as readily accessible but believes their attitudes must change in order to avail themselves of such opportunities.

For most minority students, the public schools are a foreboding place where they often feel unwelcome and alienated. Every club, extra-curricular activity, or social event poses a new, difficult challenge where they will be scrutinized, evaluated and judged. In class, subtle prejudices are often conveyed, even by well-meaning teachers. One African-American girl recounted the hurt she felt after receiving a C on a test paper. The teacher tried to reassure her by saying, "You are doing really well. I'm proud of you. Keep up the good work." But when the teacher returned a paper to a white student with a similar grade she was scolded, "You can do better than that. A C is not a good grade for you. You can do better!" Such callous remarks, however unintentional, still have a devastating impact on minority students and contribute to their general sense of not belonging in the traditional school setting.

While many black students feel that the public schools do not address their needs, Hispanic children face an entirely different set of obstacles. Over the past decades, thousands have emigrated from Central and South American countries. These students bring with them the very real trauma they have experienced throughout their young lives. Many have the added burden of having been separated from parents, family, and loved ones.

Once in the United States, language poses a major obstacle to their education. Many students are channeled into English as a Second Language (ESL) courses, where teachers diligently labor to improve their basic language skills. By taking such special courses, the students find themselves isolated from other students in the school, making it exceedingly difficult to establish new friendships.

Even when finally mainstreamed, it is difficult for Hispanic students to become involved in classes or to exert themselves because they are often embarrassed by their accent or fearful of using a poorly chosen word that could lead to ridicule by their fellow classmates. Well-meaning teachers, hoping to spare them from such mortification, only compound the problem by not calling on Hispanic students in class nor asking them to volunteer for assignments. One young girl, an immigrant from Central America, said, "They treated us like babies and gave us easy work. They thought we were not smart because we did not know much English, so we did not learn what we needed. Some of the others [students] liked that, but the teachers should have been harder."

Sheer economic necessity requires many of these students to maintain a job to help meet the financial needs of their family. They frequently work long hours at physically exhausting jobs for modest wages. Likewise, they may be expected to take on the added responsibility of caring for younger brothers and sisters, further reducing the time they have to spend on their studies. Absenteeism from school is common, while others attend school physically and mentally exhausted, unable to concentrate on their courses.

The public schools have become more aware and sensitive to the growing and diverse needs of their rapidly changing populations. Virtually all faculties now receive regular in-service training in human relations, special strategies for teaching minority students, and implementation of multicul-tural approaches in teaching their courses. At the same time, the public schools have quietly reverted to a system of group-ing students according to ability in an attempt to remediate weaker students while offering more advanced students the opportunity to pursue an accelerated curriculum. Although well-intentioned, such a system has failed to achieve the de-sired results.

Basic, remedial classes in high school have virtually reim-posed a system of segregation supposedly outlawed since the 1954 *Brown* decision. Black and Hispanic students are chan-neled too quickly into such courses, which tend only to vali-date their academic weakness and to contribute to their sense of alienation. The low intellectual level of these classes, cou-pled with primary-level textbooks and simple lessons, under-standably causes them to loath school, since they are con-stantly confronted with the stark discrepancy between their own school work and that of their peers. Students quickly identify themselves as the "dummies" in the school, accepting what the school tells them. Even graduation offers these stu-dents little hope for meaningful advancement or minimal suc-cess since most are still reading on a elementary level with few job skills. One black student recently recalled, "I find that the blacks at my high school developed a self-defeatist attitude because they thought that they could not compete with the white kids. In order to protect their self-esteem, they devel-oped a defense mechanism where they decided that they would not try, so if they failed they could say that it was because they did not want to succeed, not that they couldn't succeed. It was a way to save face." This phenomenon is most prevalent with black adolescent males who feel that, although it is acceptable for white counterparts to excel academically, it is definitely uncool for them. The energy that could be ex-erted on studies is too often channeled into sports or music, areas deemed not only admissible, but prestigious in the eyes of black youth.

Many critics of American education see ability grouping as a subtle form of racism. Diane Jones, a highly-involved black parent of two teenage boys, spoke eloquently about the need to rectify the inequities present in American schools, "The alarming trends with respect to under-achievement and failure rates of our African-American students and the concurrent drop in enrollment is a national problem of epidemic proportions which is symptomatic of a much larger failure of our society: the failure to accept each other without regard to such superficial characteristics as color or gender. Here we are in 1991, more separated in many fundamental ways than we have ever been. . . . In the Black community we have a very old expression which sums up our approach: 'Each One Teach One.' This means that we are aware that we cannot afford to lose one single mind. The United Negro College Fund reiterates this principle with its motto, 'A mind is a terrible thing to waste.' Our position in this country has always been so tenuous, now more than ever, that the development of every ability to its fullest potential remains a priority of the highest order. We see education as a cooperative process in which every ability level has something to learn from every other."

Dr. Henry Gradillas, the former principal of Garfield High School in Los Angeles, said that schools too often fail to challenge minority students or to provide them with courses that sufficiently prepare them for the future. "[Too often] because kids happen to be poor or black or Latino, they are introduced only to the lowest levels of math, called basic math. That is at the 7th or 8th grade level, sometimes not even that. Then they will not be given any math after they have finished that course. So you have a high school kid who graduates with a knowledge of math at the imbecile level. What kind of job can this person get from anybody?"

Gradillas ordered his school's guidance department to alter all student schedules to include substantive courses in algebra, computer science, and chemistry. For weaker students, a system of academic support was established to help them improve their academic performance rather than allowing them to languish in basic classes. Still, there was substantial opposition within the school to Gradillas's program. Many teachers felt that their students were incapable of learning such subjects. By resisting these changes, they were unintentionally perpetuating a cycle of failure. But after several weeks, most students rose to the academic challenge and began to experience success, many for the first time in their lives. A new tradition of high expectations and scholastic achievement began at Garfield High School. In a school that had never even offered Advanced Placement (AP) tests, over 500 such college-level examinations were administered in 1990 in a school that remains primarily Latino in its population make up.

Jaime Escalante, a nationally recognized educator who taught mathematics at Garfield, is convinced that minority students can perform better academically if only teachers, administrators, and parents establish a rigorous curriculum and encourage students by expecting success. In a pamphlet entitled *The Jaime Escalante Math Program,* he writes, "When students of any race, ethnicity, or economic status are expected to work hard, they will usually rise to the occasion, devote themselves to the task, and do the work. If we expect them to be losers they will be losers; if we expect them to be winners they will be winners. They rise, or fall, to the level of the expectations of those around them, especially their parents and their teachers."

Escalante readily admits that many minority students have outside hardships that can adversely affect their education, but he believes that such barriers are surmountable. "The children of the barrio have enormous obstacles to overcome to get an education," he writes. "Most of the families of the children I teach at Garfield have incomes below the poverty line. The majority of the parents have not been to college—frequently, Mom and Dad have never even been to high school—

and they may or may not appreciate the long-term value of education. Many do not know how to provide a supportive atmosphere for the serious student, and often they may require the child to get a job to help support the family. Teen pregnancy, drugs, and the stresses upon single-parent homes are all terribly real problems for these students. Gangs operate freely in their neighborhoods. Are my students affected by these barriers? Of course. Are my students victims of these barriers? No. The educational process begins at this point." Henry Gradillas agrees claiming, "all kids are going to have problems in life but why compound that by giving them another handicap and not educate them?"

Increasingly, high school principals and school superintendents have begun to recognize the pressing need to revamp secondary school curricula to provide minority students with more substantive classes, especially in mathematics and sciences. Dr. Paul Vance, the first black superintendent of Montgomery County in Maryland, maintained in a recent newspaper interview, that if all students successfully completed Algebra and similar academic courses, ". . . there would be no barriers to the children of color. And there would be no erratic test reports." Kathy Kirk, a teacher in the system, agreed with the superintendent maintaining, "When students were allowed to take the easy, basic math courses, not only did they never reach the level of competency to take geometry, trigonometry, or calculus, which are needed for college, they also were prevented from taking chemistry or physics because they lacked the math skills to handle them. The lack of higher level math knocked them out of participation in two academic areas."

While few would argue over the need for improving minority students' math and science proficiency, there is little consensus on what should be taught in English, history, or humanities classes. Many increasingly outspoken critics of American education have charged that such subjects reflect only the majority culture. The focus, they maintain, is on European and western culture, while ignoring the equally valuable and important contributions of people of color. As a result, these activists have given up on any meaningful reform and have instead demanded the institution of an exclusively Afrocentric curriculum designed to inspire black students and to instill racial pride. Classes teach African civilization, culture, history, music, and art, but are equally limited in their perspective. Questionable historical analysis and interpretation have led to valid charges that the curriculum is more political than academic. By isolating ethnic groups and emphasizing differences, the United States is at risk of becoming the Yugoslavia of the Western hemisphere, divided and fragmented with little sense of national identity.

While Afrocentric courses are divisive in their approach, a multicultural curriculum of history and literature fairly credits the many contributions of all cultures. According to Gladys McClain, the assistant principal of Bethesda-Chevy Chase High School, "We need more black writers and black history taught in high schools. For history [as it has been traditionally taught] to be so myopic is degrading. I would hate, though, to see us go to an extreme saying that [only] black or Hispanic history or literature should be taught, so that we become myopic in a different direction. We all need to see history from all the different perspectives and viewpoints. I prefer the multicultural approach to be part of the curriculum rather than a little taught in January for Dr. Martin Luther King's birthday or February for Black History Month. We do it then and do it happily because that has been all we have had, but I think it would be better if it were important in the teaching of overall history."

Diane Ravitch and Chester Finn, in a recent PBS special on the problems of American education, likewise argued for a multicultural approach by likening American history and culture to a rich mosaic of multicolored tiles. But they cautioned that it was imperative to study the entire mosaic along with the glue that holds the mosaic together to gain an accurate perspective. Diane Ravitch went on to argue that while it is important for all people to study their own individual ethnic backgrounds, no one should "lose sight of the fact that you are part of a country and not just a racial or ethnic group. If you only study the history of one segment of this country, you're not educating yourself to live in America in the 21st century."

The validity of studying the contributions of various civilizations, ethnic groups, and individuals is clearly illustrated by the life of Martin Luther King. In an essay entitled, "Teaching Tips on Martin Luther King, Jr.", Mertha R. Johnson, a humanities teacher from Georgia, writes, "The writings of Dr. King transcend various canons of knowledge. His treatise on civil disobedience is a universal theme echoed in the works of Sophocles and the writings of David Thoreau. His principles of nonviolence find expression through his mentor, Mahatma Ghandi, the wisdom literature, plain of ancient Egypt, Biblical history and literature, and strains of American transcendentalism. The sources of Dr. King's philosophy exist in Greek, Hebrew, Hindu, and German literature. His concept of nonviolence is rooted in the doctrine of spiritual ascendancy found in Plato's 'symposium'. Dr. King was a scholar personified. He was an enlightened intellectual and should be presented to students as such." Students provided with the same broad base of knowledge could ask for little better preparation for living in an increasingly diverse world. Multicultural education has the potential to teach all students respect for others and the contributions of many to the common culture. Universal lessons of discipline, diligence, and dignity are lessons to be learned by all as they are not linked exclusively to one race or culture.

While educators continue to debate curriculum and argue over course content, many of the most important keys to improving minority achievement are being ignored. As with all students, minority parents are a crucial element in the overall effectiveness of public schools. An interested, active, and highly involved parental community is pivotal in ensuring the success of minority students as illustrated at Benjamin Mays High School in Atlanta. In a school composed primarily of black students, a powerful coalition between school and home was established through the exceptional efforts of the principal, Ruby McClendon. She explained, "We have a lot of involvement with our parents. We have parent volunteers and we get information about what kinds of jobs they have and if they can come help us in any way, even if it is just for thirty minutes a week. Consequently, we have parents coming in and out of the school, and once they start to do that they feel, more of a belonging, more of a closeness, as this is our school and they refer to it that way. It makes an impact not just on the students, but on everyone. The students don't know when they may run into their parents in the hallways and they get the support they need. Parents help in many ways—to file, make phone calls, or assist teachers. . . . The parents and the students must know that the learning process and the teaching process rests not just with the school, but with the entire community. We try to get everyone to buy ownership in the entire program. When we do this we have a lot of people on our team."

Parents, teachers, and administrators can form an imposing alliance by simultaneously increasing academic expectations for students and working to instill pride in scholastic achievement. These critical attitudinal changes have a major, positive impact on a school's overall learning environment by making students accountable for their studies and behavior. Mrs. McClendon explained, "We have a job to show the students that we are interested in everyone, that we expect everyone to succeed, that we have a program for everyone, and that we want everyone to be involved with each other. . . . We have high standards for everybody, particularly as far as behavior is concerned. I tell the students that I feel badly about punishing anybody, but I don't feel badly when I have already told them what I expect. If I am certain that I have already told them clearly, then I am just as certain that if they break the rules and regulations that they will take the consequences. They are going to take them like young men and young ladies because they knew ahead of time what the results would be."

At the same time, students are constantly encouraged to take pride in their school and in themselves. At Benjamin Mays, students have been encouraged to become involved in setting the school's goals and working with the faculty and administration to improve learning conditions. "There must be some empowerment of our students," McClendon asserted. "We try to make them independent thinkers, and by doing that we allow them to be involved in the goal-setting, the decision-making and the plan for their educational life here at Mays."

In an effort to further increase student involvement in the daily workings of the school, so-called "rap sessions" between students and counselors were initiated. Here students could freely explore topics of interest as well as debate various issues that involved personal values. Mrs. McClendon explained, "We are very interested in clarifying values with the students. We see the need for a set of positive values for the students, so we do as many value-clarification activities as we can. Guidance counselors set up rap sessions with the students and with local educators and business persons and they talk about values." One such productive activity explored what would be required to establish an ideal school for students. Mrs. McClendon said that the students universally talked about, ". . . good attendance and being respectful; courtesy, good temperament, and helping one another." They felt that a model school would have ". . . teachers who were caring, who showed students they really wanted them to learn by giving them focus and direction" while parents would give moral support to their children and "be home more and be involved by having good communication with the schools." Mays students also believed that the principal in charge of the school should "know a large percentage of the students and that students should feel they were able to approach the principal" who would maintain a high visibility and be accessible.

Teachers are also a vital part of the complex equation for improving the performance of minority students. For many minority students, teachers represent an authoritarian force and are people who are either feared or avoided. Many students complain of having little rapport with their teachers. One black parent explained this pervasive feeling among minority teenagers, "Students often remember a teacher who has made a difference for them, but many of the black kids cannot remember a single teacher who cared or pushed them and said, 'I know you can do this.' As a result, sometimes black kids feel like, 'I am going to make it miserable for you because you don't want me here anyway.' The reason they feel like that is that they have gotten the message loud and clear that they are not wanted. That is then their defense."

Schools which have had proven success in teaching minority students invariably have assembled a committed, dedicated faculty determined to help each student succeed. These earnest teachers maintain their high academic standards and expectations but are also willing to get involved in helping their students cope with school, personal problems, and other difficulties. Diane Breakiron, the 1991 Fairfax County Teacher of the Year, teaches science at J.E.B. Stuart High School in Virginia. The school has students from over sixty countries and many of the teenagers have only limited language skills.

Breakiron believes that great strides can be made in improving the achievement of Hispanic students if teachers take extra steps to understand cultural differences and then to offer special support for students in need. Breakiron said, "One of the problems is that too many teachers see anybody who speaks Spanish as Hispanic. It matters very much to the students that a teacher knows where they are from and cares about the differences between nationalities." She discovered that her students were not a monolithic group, but from diverse cultures with distinct characteristics. "Sometimes students would not work with others of different background or even sit near them. I found it difficult to reach some of them."

In order to become more effective with Hispanic students Breakiron enrolled in a Spanish for Educators class. "It wasn't until I took that class . . . that I found a way to reach them. The students saw me trying to speak the language, they helped me with my dialogues . . . that helped to cement our relationship."

According to Breakiron, the most beneficial results occurred when, "I check their attendance and help them with homework just like a parent is supposed to. I help them with reports, listen to problems, take them to the library, just like a parent. This is a way to give the students the parental involvement they do not get because their own parent does not understand the [school] system and does not participate." Another teacher agreed and said, "Hispanic parents have the attitude that school personnel are on a different plane and they know best, so the parent does not interfere. It is important to realize that this is respect, but it is not a helpful attitude at all."

Breakiron sees a different agenda at work for certain minority groups. "Black parents are more cognizant of what the American school system involves, so if the teacher calls to talk to them or they come to school for a conference, they have had some personal experience with it. They then react differently to their children than the Hispanic parents who may have no education themselves and have no familiarity with the school system. Hispanic parents are intimidated by the schools and do not want to become a part of the process, so it is hard to reach their children.

"I did not go into teaching to parent, but I have come to realize that unless I am ready to parent, I cannot teach. I cannot have my kids succeed." Breakiron, although highly successful with minority students, does not limit her "parenting" techniques to a select group. She said, "All kids are at risk. Every kid is at risk and that is why I do not like labels like at-risk or minority or non-minority. Every kid that comes through high school needs extra support."

Most teachers, however, faced with their own family commitments and responsibilities, are constrained from devoting such large amount of time to students outside the classroom. Still, they do have the ability to positively affect minority students. Gladys McClain believes that good teachers who maintain high standards and who are genuinely interested in a child's welfare can make a difference. She explained, "The teacher has to be a caring person. Minority students know if a teacher cares. If a teacher works them hard, they know that the teacher probably cares more than everybody else. The teacher who really makes an impression is the one who holds the line, that sets some standards, that really cares—that cares so much that she will call a parent and take the risk of the student being angry at them to get some communication going with the family. The students know these teachers care."

Many teachers, fearful that such efforts will lead to confrontations with minority students, are petrified at being labeled racists. They avoid such criticism by developing separate, less challenging standards for some students as a means of avoiding conflict. Mrs. McClain believes that such teachers are unknowingly inflicting harm on students and should have the courage to do what they know to be educationally right, "Sometimes people are afraid to say things that are right and that are true for fear of stepping on someone's toes. Any teacher who cares enough to say, 'I know you can do better than this. I know your parents have better expectations for you and I have better expectations for you. I expect to see a turn-around.' And the teachers will see a turn-around." Teachers must take risks to help those at risk. The truth is that fair, reasonable academic standards rarely bring charges of unfairness, nor will minority students react negatively to such demands. McClain continued, "Too many teachers do just the bare minimum and are not extending themselves. There comes a time when a teacher has to go beyond what they would normally do. The teacher has to be a caring person [to be effective in today's schools]."

Ruby McClendon agrees that a school's faculty must be committed to improving student achievement. "We try to ensure that our school personnel are committed to the success of students and that requires on-going staff development for the faculty, so that we know our reason for being here is to guarantee the success of students. Students sometimes feel that teachers do not care if the student makes an *F*. We have to make sure that the school personnel are committed to not letting them fail."

There is no excuse for the continuing failure of the American educational system to adequately address the needs of minority youngsters. For the past decade the achievement levels of black and Hispanic students have been studied, analyzed, and debated. Dropout rates are still appalling and test scores are intolerably low. The answer to improving minority academic achievement rests with maintaining high expectations and conveying the belief that they will succeed.

Minority students constitute a vast, untapped resource in the United States. Remedies do exist, however, to engage these young people and enable them to flourish academically. The power to improve achievement lies in the hands of teachers, parents, and students. Success can take place if stereotypes are put aside and high expectations are held for all students. Teachers can encourage young people to realize their potential by genuinely caring about all of America's youth, expecting great things from all students, and extending themselves to provide the support and means by which young people can learn. School curriculum can reflect the great diversity of this country through a multicultural course of study revealing the contributions of all Americans. Parents can become actively involved and vigilant as they take charge of their child's academic fate. Students who commit themselves to hard work and determined effort can excel if they avoid the destructive attitudes and influences in today's society that will only lead to academic defeat.

When America's schools clearly recognize the value of all their students and strive for the success of the entire population, change can take place. One of the first steps is in setting appropriate expectations for all students. Former Secretary of Education William Bennett says, "If we expect failure, we are going to get failure, if we focus on success we are going to get success." Success is contagious and as expectations concerning American education shift, achievement will become more readily accessible to a much larger and more varied group of young people. Through a united effort, teachers, parents and students can advance the common goal of confirming that education is the universal key to future success.

Chapter
Eight

A "Special Interest" in Education

"This institution will be based on the illimitable freedom of the human mind. For here we are not afraid to follow truth wherever it may lead, nor to tolerate any error so long as reason is left free to combat it."

THOMAS JEFFERSON

IN MOBILE, ALABAMA, ONE PARENT complained to school authorities that J.R.R. Tolkien's epic fantasy, *The Hobbit,* promoted Satanism and demanded that it be immediately removed from a junior high school's library. A substitute teacher in California protested a teacher's lesson on the holocaust claiming that "our students have enough horrible things in their lives without studying this." In another California school district, English teachers were charged with racism for using Mark Twain's *The Adventures of Huckleberry Finn* in sophomore literature classes. Elsewhere, the People for the Ethical Treatment of Animals has launched a nationwide effort to ban all dissection of laboratory animals in high school science classes, while AIDS activists convinced New York City public school officials to adopt a condom distribution program for its 261,000 high school students. The schools have become a modern political battleground with partisan extremists, fanatical zealots, and radical activists all organized in a concerted effort to apply pressure on the public schools in an effort to advance an ideological, philosophical, or moral viewpoint. They have launched a virulent assault on the established academic curricula leading to 244 documented cases of academic censorship in the nation's public schools in 1990 alone. The result of the relentless and brutal attack on public schools has been the loss of the traditional consensus concerning what to teach American students, and serves only to add a vast array of conflicting social schemes to the nation's already crowded educational agenda.

The modern special interest groups span the ideological spectrum from liberal to conservative. Some are concerned about having lessons concerning contraception included in health classes while others want to re-institute daily prayer. The one thing they all have in common, though, is that they are only concerned with advancing their own individual causes by lobbying local school boards and exerting political pressure. The policy makers for the schools, in an effort to mollify and appease these groups, increasingly choose to make curriculum decisions based upon expediency rather than academic merit. According to journalist William Henry, "Curriculums are being written to satisfy the political demands of parents and community activists. In some cases, expediency counts for more than facts. New York State officials, for example, have responded to pressure from Native American leaders by revamping the state high school curriculum to include the shaky assertion that the U.S. Constitution was based on the political system of the Iroquois Confederacy. . . . The chief risk in any ideologically based curriculum is that it can promote tribalism and downplay the value of discovering common cultural ground. The very idea of the melting pot, of assimilation, indeed of a common American identity, is under fire in some academic circles."

The loss of general consensus on the purpose and goals of American education has contributed to a steady decline in student verbal and math scores on the Scholastic Aptitude

Test (SAT), culminating in a 20 year low in 1990 with a combined national average of just 896. Far more serious than student test performance, though, is the woeful ignorance of the average high school graduate of even the most basic elements of American history, culture, and literature. Professor E.D. Hirsch of the University of Virginia writes in his book, *Cultural Literacy,* ". . . two-thirds of our seventeen-year-olds do not know that the Civil War occurred between 1850 and 1900. Three quarters do not know what *reconstruction* means. Half do not know the meaning of the *Brown decision* and cannot identify either Stalin or Churchill. Three-quarters are unfamiliar with the names of standard American and British authors. Moreover, our seventeen-year-olds have little sense of geography or the relative chronology of major events. Reports of youthful ignorance can no longer be considered merely impressionistic."

Despite this abysmal failure, special interest groups remain unrelenting in their steadfast determination to undermine traditional education. Twentieth-century sociological standards and values are inappropriately applied to the past for modern political purposes in an effort to expose historical racism, exploitation, and prejudice. The motives of writers, explorers, presidents, and patriots are inevitably reduced to a vague but universal historical conspiracy intent upon exploiting the lower class and victimizing women, minorities, and the disadvantaged. Thus, Christopher Columbus arrived in the New World not as a courageous explorer, but rather as a white European determined to inflict genocide on the passive, peaceful American Indian; Thomas Jefferson, the author of the Declaration of Independence, is no longer an enlightened political philosopher, but merely another hypocritical slave holder; and even Jim and Huck's expedition down the Mississippi River is transformed into a thinly-disguised homosexual voyage. Although most responsible teachers continue to denounce such assertions as nonsense, course content is quietly being modified to satisfy the outside zealots and political activists, with classroom teachers voluntarily purging their courses of any subject matter that may lead to controversy or criticism.

Former Secretary of Education, William Bennett, argues that the recent trends in American education have been an aberration and are not reflective of the attitudes of the general populace. Bennett maintains, "The first thing to realize is that [such trends are] a drift. This is a departing from what most of the people want and want to see happen [in the schools] . . . We have had a fundamental disagreement about what school is for. I kept repeating the Gallup poll—teach our children how to speak, write, read, count, think, help them develop reliable standards of right and wrong that will guide them through life. [State superintendents] kept talking about preparing students for the 21st century, joining a multicultural, interdependent world, life adjustments. . . . If you don't agree on the purposes, you're not going to get the means right, you are not going to agree on curriculum.

"I think the main purpose here is to make kids smarter. And one [teacher] said, 'But that may not lead to the reform of society.' I said, 'That is none of your business. It is not what you are hired to do. You are hired to make that kid smarter— to know his culture, to know his geography, to know his math, his science.' It is a fundamental disagreement.

"I think [the drift] had a lot to do with what was going on in the 60's and 70's. I think there was a turn when I found that, in the schools, traditional became synonymous with bad and innovative synonymous with good. So the way we used to do it was wrong and the new way was at least worth trying. And the burden of proof fell on all those things which had time-honored practices and there wasn't as much burden of proof on the new stuff. It was a major cultural shift. The interesting thing is that the American people didn't change but those people, organizations, and institutions whose leadership had a great deal to do with what was going on in the schools, they shifted. And that accounts for the discrepancy.

"We've tended to drift away from the basic disciplines. . . . I did a survey when I was at the National Endowment for the Humanities. I asked 250 influential Americans what ten books every high school graduate in America should be familiar with by the time he or she leaves the school. I sent it to liberals, conservatives, blacks, whites, Republicans, Democrats, across the spectrum. . . . I got a lot of different opinions but what was interesting was that there was consensus on four—Shakespeare, the Bible, some guiding documents such as the *Federalist Papers,* the Constitution, the Declaration, the Emancipation, and the great American novel—*Huckleberry Finn* . . . George Will reprinted my request in his column and got about 600 responses which he sent to me. The public that was reading George Will's column, had the same view as the 250 people . . . these books kept appearing. . . . Whether you regard [a particular work] as your friend or your enemy, no one can argue the influence of those books."

Despite the pressing and obvious need for some general agreement on curriculum, American education remains hopelessly fragmented with each of the fifty states and literally thousands of individual school districts pursuing a different agenda and separate goals. State legislatures, county school boards, local curriculum specialists, Parent-Teacher Associations, ideological interest groups, political activists, school principals, and even individual citizens, all demand input into what is actually being taught in today's classrooms. Increasingly, the emphasis has been shifted from course content and core knowledge to improving student interaction with each other and to attaining broad (but not clearly defined) sociological objectives. High school courses have become more eclectic with class titles giving little insight into what is actually being taught. In many jurisdictions, American literature classes ignore even the most fundamental writers and poets in a never ending quest for relevancy and multiculturalism. History classes, likewise, have degenerated into a hodgepodge of seemingly unrelated themes without any effort at continuity or

DOONESBURY copyright 1988 G.B. Trudeau. Reprinted with permission of Universal Press Syndicate. All rights reserved.

chronology. Lynne Cheney, the chairman of the National Endowment for the Humanities, explains: "What I despair about is being able to go from Georgia to Minneapolis to California and not be able to find a single book that everyone has read. It is the whole idea of common culture that we are losing. . . . Everyone should read Shakespeare and everyone should read Martin Luther King, too. But we do need to work towards some effort to have a unified understanding of what literature should include. What are the things that every student ought to read no matter who she or he is? Students who are white and live in [affluent suburbs] should read Toni Morrison's [stories of the black experience]. And kids who happen to be African-American and live in an urban area should read Shakespeare. That kind of consensus has just broken down."

Various interest groups have made access to high school students a major priority since their extremist messages are more readily accepted by unquestioning young minds which are more susceptible to emotional appeals. But in such cases, education no longer serves as a tool of enlightenment, but rather a lethal weapon of political ideology. Thomas Sowell of the Hoover Institute in California writes, "There are the 'peace studies' or 'nuclear education' programs in which the horrors of war are presented so graphically and so relentlessly that many children are reduced to tears. One teacher told her seventh-grade students that 'No one in this class will be alive in the year 2000.' What all of these programs have in common is that zealots are out to promote their own fads or causes to a captive audience of vulnerable children. The emotional well-being of these children is not their problem. How do they get away with it? Deception is crucial."

In suburban Maryland, *Washington Post* columnist Colman McCarthy offers one such course at a local high school. The class, innocuously entitled "Alternatives to Violence," was never approved or evaluated by the county school board despite rigorous requirements for all new course offerings. Instead, to avoid detection, it was first camouflaged under existing course numbers, as "Social Studies Internship" and later simply as "Philosophy." McCarthy's class, however, bore no resemblance to the search for truth and the pursuit of wisdom originated by Plato, Aristotle, and Socrates. Indeed, one individual intimately familiar with McCarthy's tactics and teaching methods claimed that to list the course as philosophy was tantamount to outright fraud. He explained, "I would call it a lie. When a college goes to look at that transcript, they are going to think that this child has studied philosophy, studied philosophers, knows about the different writers of eastern and western thought. And that is not true. The only thing they are going to know about is the one-sided view of a columnist."

Since McCarthy lacked the state-mandated teaching credentials required to work in the public schools, a licensed teacher was detailed to sit daily in the class to fulfill the letter if not the spirit of local laws. Still, the course failed to meet even minimal academic standards since there was no established curriculum, written objectives, or detailed lesson plans. Rather the class served as McCarthy's personal forum to denounce the government, its political leaders, and virtually all of the school's educational policies from grades to attendance, much to the delight of his enraptured student audience. One staff member recalled, "He said he doesn't believe in grades or attendance. Those type of things weren't right. Schools shouldn't force people to come . . . these things don't have any relevance to the educational process and are actually detrimental. He went on to say he was an anarchist and did not believe in laws."

Each day, McCarthy ranted and raved against everything from traffic lights to American foreign policy. He even conspired against other teachers and their efforts by encouraging students to wage "homework strikes" in their courses. One of his most passionate discourses was devoted exclusively to condemning the study of science and math in high school despite a county-wide objective to improve student performance in those subject areas. Over a newspaper headline reporting such efforts, McCarthy had scrawled the theme for one lesson, "Gist—Science and Math are not good. What is one good thing a scientist or math person has made/done?" He later expounded upon this ridiculous premise in a *Washington Post* editorial claiming, "Algebra isn't essential to much of anything. Once adding, subtracting, multiplying and dividing are mastered—by eighth grade usually—why insist on more?. . . . The few keep torturing the most. . . . Algebra is more loathed than learned, more endured than embraced. It is more memorized to pass tests than understood to comprehend problems. . . . I happen to think that algebra is a useless torture. I have never seen a help-wanted ad for an algebraist, and in 25 years of interviewing I have not met anyone who even mentioned algebra, let alone said it was beneficial." Such a message, no matter how ridiculous, served to undermine the extensive efforts of the school's math department and reaffirmed the misconception of students that what their other instructors were teaching was worthless to their academic development.

When some students boldly attempted to exert their independence by questioning why other opinions on various controversial issues were never discussed, McCarthy cavalierly dismissed the criticism with the absurd claim that he was under no obligation, morally or legally, to present alternative viewpoints. The American judiciary, though, has consistently ruled otherwise concluding that the public schools cannot be used by zealots to indoctrinate students. In *Knarr vs. the Board of Education,* the courts established the principle that the public schools cannot be used to "sway and influence the minds of young people without a full and proper explanation of both sides of the issue." Furthermore, in a November 1990 ruling, the U.S. Court of Appeals stated that "The First Amendment is not a teacher license for uncontrolled expression at variance with established curricular content." These clear judicial statements, however, did little to deter Mc-

Carthy in his efforts to cultivate a crop of loyal, unquestioning disciples.

Such direct access to students, though, is rarely open to most special interest groups. Instead, the textbook selection process offers an even more promising way to influence what is being taught in the public schools. The adoption of textbooks for student use represents a crucial financial and philosophical commitment by a school system since such texts will be in continual use for a minimum of five years without any substantive alteration or addendum. National textbook publishers are eager to tap the lucrative educational market, worth millions of dollars, and aggressively compete with each other to produce a suitable book that will meet the often diverse curriculum demands of state and local committees. Yet they, too, are frustrated by the seemingly endless list of conflicting and contradictory requirements.

In 22 states, including the population giants of Texas and California, a centralized textbook adoption process is used. The remaining states empower local school districts to choose their own books to support a state-mandated curriculum. The special interests have targeted this selection process for political activism, particularly when it involves the history, literature, and science curricula. Interest groups demand that school-adopted textbooks adequately reflect their own special agenda while excluding other, divergent view points. Thus, fundamentalists insist that the doctrine of Creationism supplant the theory of evolution; minority groups press for more ethnic history and culture and fewer Anglo-Saxons; and feminists argue for more women's literature and less Hemingway.

The public hearings that are conducted by textbook selection committees to solicit citizen opinion and to engage in reasonable and scholarly discourse, have degenerated into bitter and divisive forums with contending parties freely trading epithets impugning the integrity and motives of teachers, administrators, board members, and other rival groups. In California, which accounts for 11 percent of all textbook purchases, a state-wide task force developed an innovative and far-reaching social studies program designed to improve student geography skills, historical knowledge, and appreciation of various cultures. The textbooks which were finally approved were excellent. They had a multi-cultural approach, well-written prose, and high-quality lessons. Still they were denounced and brutally attacked by organized special interest groups. According to Stephan Goode in an article for *Insight* magazine, "The loudest criticisms have come from minority groups who claim to have been excluded from the textbooks, or who demand changes they think are needed to treat their own history seriously. Jewish groups, for example, protested that one of the books describes judges at Jesus Christ's trial as Jewish, reviving memories of centuries of accusations by certain Christians that Jews were responsible for Christ's crucifixion. Gay and lesbian advocates have complained that the texts ignore homosexuals in history. The loudest protests came from blacks, such as Joyce E. King . . . [who] found the whole endeavor European-oriented and white-centered. . . . There were demands, for example, that ancient Egypt be recognized as a black civilization, a point that is fiercely debated by many historians." Interest group inclusion has now become far more important than historical fact or scholarship in the increasingly bitter textbook debate.

In a desperate effort to avoid educational stalemate, textbook selection committees have repeatedly opted for bland books that de-emphasize content. They have also forsaken legitimate scholarship by attempting to objectify the process by using elaborate check lists designed to placate various interest groups. Former Secretary of Education, William Bennett, in *American Education: Making it Work,* explains: "Women, ethnic minorities, environmentalists, the elderly, the handicapped—even nutritionists—all demand that textbooks present their interests fairly. That's reasonable enough. But again, state and local agencies too often use crude formulae in an attempt to guarantee appropriate 'social content.'

They count the number of women in a book's photographs or the number of Catholics mentioned in its text. Or they may publish lists of items and ideas meant to be emphasized or down-played. Until 1986, for example, California took a dim view of books with photographs of luncheon meat or butter because these items have too much fat and too much salt. This approach to textbook selection opens well-meaning efforts and deserving causes to ridicule. And more important, it denigrates and unnecessarily complicates an already difficult task—the provision of high quality books to our school children."

Textbook publishers have bowed to interest group pressure by generating dull and uninspired books, fearful that any perceived controversy will lessen their chance for adoption. They have camouflaged the lack of academic substance and scholarship by making their books highly visual with colorful photographs, elaborate charts, detailed graphs, and impressive layouts. But as Lynne Cheney aptly points out in *Tyrannical Machines,* "Many textbooks used in American schools are so dull that no one would read them voluntarily." Indeed, high school students simply deposit many of their assigned textbooks in their school lockers and leave them there, unread and unstudied, until they are forced to return them at the end of the school year.

Much of the vibrancy of an academic subject is lost with these uninspired books. Biology, chemistry, and mathematics seem to have little relevancy while American history is reduced to a series of seemingly unrelated statistics, blurred faces, and meaningless facts. Former principal Bob Eikel, argues that modern textbooks undermine the curriculum. He recalled that when one county adopted a world history textbook, "Two women artists in the Renaissance who nobody ever heard of [were included] but Vermeer and Franz Hals were left out. If they didn't do anything that anybody ever heard of, why put them in there to make somebody feel good?" In the same school district, the county-mandated American history textbook devoted only three scant paragraphs to the entire Vietnam conflict despite its importance and its high interest level for modern students. Little wonder that young people soon lose all sense of drama, human progress, and historical significance.

High school American literature anthologies fare little better, scrupulously avoiding such important Puritan writers and thinkers as William Bradford, Cotton Mather, and Anne Bradstreet and any meaningful discussion of religion and its impact on early America. Even those writers fortunate enough to be included in literature books are carefully censored and sanitized. Lynne Cheney writes, "Literature has also felt the effect of publishers' desire to avoid controversy. Author Ray Bradbury has recounted one publishing house's attempt to remove religious references from 'The Fog Horn,' a short story in which he described the illumination coming from a lighthouse as a 'God-Light.' Those seeing the light from a sea creature's perspective, Bradbury wrote in the story, would have felt they were in 'the Presence.' Editors who wanted to include 'the Fog Horn' in a high school anthology deleted both 'God Light' and 'the Presence.' *Fahrenheit 451,* Bradbury's novel about censorship and book burning, has also been censored. Unbeknownst to him, editors over the years deleted some seventy-five separate sections they judged might cause offense."

Supplementary books and even the school's library holdings have similarly come under assault by the special interests. According to a recent survey conducted by the People for the American Way, John Steinbeck's *Of Mice and Men,* J.D. Salinger's *The Catcher in the Rye,* and Mark Twain's *The Adventures of Huckleberry Finn* were among the most challenged books that are traditionally taught in America's public schools. Yet throughout the United States, other incidents of public pressure to impose censorship abound. In Maryland, several parents lobbied to have Shakespeare's *Romeo and Juliet* eliminated from the high school curriculum on the dubious grounds that in promoted teen suicide. Dr. Seuss's children's story, *The Lorax,* which promotes conservation and concern for the environment, was condemned in California as being anti-logging while other critics reduced Charles Dickens' classic fable, *A Christmas Story,* to a dangerous and corrupting story of demons and ghosts. Many teachers have responded to such reckless and ruthless political attacks with self-imposed censorship, refusing to teach any book that could possibly spark controversy. Yet, by doing so, they also deny their students the opportunity to read and experience some of the world's great literature.

Few books have caused more public ire than *The Adventures of Huckleberry Finn.* When Mark Twain first published the book in 1885, the nation's school teachers universally condemned it for its poor grammar and tried to dissuade students from reading it, fearing they would emulate Huck's limited vocabulary. In more recent years, modern, but equally ill-informed critics, have charged that the book is racist and should thus be withdrawn from the secondary school curriculum. John C. Gerber, an emeritus professor of English at the University of Iowa, writes in *One Hundred Years of Huckleberry Finn,* ". . . English teachers have had to contend with organized groups that wanted the book banned from the curriculum. . . . Although formal protests against the book in such states as Texas, New York, Virginia, and Iowa have been set aside, no one knows how many teachers have quietly taken *Huckleberry Finn* off their reading lists, either because they agree with the protestors or because they want to avoid possible trouble."

In 1982, a school administrator, ironically at Mark Twain Intermediate School in Fairfax County, Virginia, launched a ruthless assault on the legitimacy of *Huckleberry Finn* claiming, "The book is poison. It is anti-American; it works against the melting pot theory of our country; it works against the idea that all men are created equal; it works against the 14th Amendment to the Constitution and against the Preamble that guarantees life, liberty, and the pursuit of happiness

[sic]." Despite such emotional and demagogic appeals, the school system wisely resisted the intense pressure to eliminate the book from the students' educational experience recognizing that such books are not merely read in the classroom but are carefully taught within the context of the curriculum. A teacher is hired as a skilled professional to provide guidance and insight to help guide students in their understanding and appreciation of an author's work. *Huckleberry Finn,* thus, is not the racist novel depicted by some ill-informed critics but rather a true classic in American literature—the first book to effectively use native American dialect and vernacular; the first American work to portray a teenage boy as the protagonist of a story; and a poignant satire of societal values common during the *antebellum* era.

The special interests, however, refuse to accept all academic arguments or to debate scholastic merit since dialogue tends to dilute the emotional appeal of their political agenda. An author's insight, talent, and impact on society must be the *foremost* factors in determining whether or not to include a work in the high school curriculum, not race, gender, or sexual persuasion. These are the reasons that teachers incorporate Charlotte Bronte's writings rather than those of romance novelist Danielle Steele.

In American education today, the political concerns of the special interests have come to dominate the academic agenda and are having an increasing influence on what is being taught in the public schools. This lamentable trend has led to the fragmentation of the schools and needs to be replaced by a restoration of a common, national consensus. Educational decisions need to be based upon what will be truly beneficial to students and curriculum decisions should be made accordingly. Furthermore, the concept of an American culture is neither to be feared nor disavowed for it is truly a rich amalgamation of various ethnic, religious, and racial heritages—one that includes the writings of George Washington and Frederick Douglass; the books of Mark Twain and Alice

Walker; the teachings of Jonathan Edwards and Malcolm X; and the history of the pioneers and Native Americans. The challenge for American education remains: to teach an appreciation of this culture and its special, universal relationship to all of its citizens. Senator Daniel Inouye of Hawaii, a highly decorated World War II veteran of Japanese descent, recounted in a book entitled *A Special Relationship,* how one of his teachers was successful in conveying just such an idea: "I came to believe that the giants who made history were *my* forefathers. Always before, I had been a little embarrassed singing about the 'land where my fathers died,' and I always spoke of *the* fathers of *the* country. It was [my teacher] who, in some wonderful subtle way convinced me of the essential relationship between America's Founding Fathers and all of the American people."

Although the special interests would surely disagree, their narrow, ideological agendas cannot be allowed to fragment and destroy the valid academic missions of the public schools. Indeed, as lawyer David Remes states in *Teacher Magazine,* "Public education is not 'public' just because it is free. It is 'public' because it is a *kind* of education—an education that instructs children, as Justice William J. Brennan has put it, in 'a common heritage to all American groups and religions.' That heritage is one that includes *The Diary of Anne Frank* and *Huckleberry Finn.* It is a heritage of tolerance and diversity. Public education is not and cannot be an education that instructs children in the orthodoxies of their parents." Likewise, novelist James Michener writes, "The school is the only agency legally established by organized society and supported by taxation whose sole job it is to teach the child knowledge, [and] the skills and values required for a successful adult life within the bounds of society." Only when this mission is clearly defined and accepted, free from politics and personal prejudice, will the schools truly be able to effectively educate America's young.

Chapter
Nine

Time Out

For Sports

"Education has got to be the first thing in our schools. We are creating a bunch of gladiators. We love to see them play, and they are fun to watch. They add a quality to our lives. But we are really taking an awful lot of things out of their lives."

JOE PATERNO
FOOTBALL COACH—PENN STATE UNIVERSITY

AMERICANS ARE OBSESSED WITH SPORTS. Not surprisingly, the American high school student is no exception. Across the country millions of youngsters are involved in organized sports of one kind or another, from Little League baseball to high school interscholastic sports. Although some will find great success from a life dedicated to sports, the sad fact is, that while the high school athlete dreams of glory on the basketball courts or the football field, few will ever achieve the dream of sports stardom in college or the pros. Meanwhile, many high school students relentlessly pursue a time-consuming and elusive goal at the expense of their education.

The benefits of participation in sports can be great. The health advantages, discipline, and sportsmanship gained from athletics can greatly enrich a student's life if the player, parents, coaches, and schools keep high school athletics in proper perspective. As long as educators use an athletic program to enhance the educational process, the athlete and school as a whole benefits. When athletics attain an exaggerated importance, the athlete is harmed and the educational system is weakened. Unfortunately, this happens all too often as the pursuit of athletic excellence gets in the way of the pursuit of academic excellence.

The message has been successfully sent to American youth that the fastest and most rewarding route to fame, glory, and big money is in the sports arena. American high schools promote that idea through their treatment of sports and athletes in the school setting. Academics in some high schools take a back seat to athletics and the attention paid to a fine scholar comes nowhere close to that given a star player.

High school students are wooed by the glitzy image they view on television of glory and fame, and find it difficult to keep sports in proper perspective in their lives. They read about astronomical salaries earned by individuals who "play games" for a living. Newspaper headlines celebrate a college junior signing a $26.5 million contract to play in the remote reaches of the Canadian Football League, while even a mediocre pro baseball player averages $891,188 per year. Black youths are especially susceptible to the lure of the money and fame as, for many, their options are fewer than their white counterparts. It is no surprise that many youths see athletics as the key to their future success and unrealistically invest all their time and energy striving to be a sports hero at the expense of their educations. The unfortunate fact is that success will escape all but the very few.

The incredible influence of high profile pro athletes on youths can have extremely damaging effects. Philip Hoose, author of *Hoosiers* and *Necessities,* said in an interview, "A lot of kids can't think of another thing to do with their lives, especially if they watch a lot of television. Pro sports players, black athletes especially, act as a terrific distraction as powerful role models." Marveling at the prowess of Michael Jordan is one thing, but teenagers unrealistically think that someday they will be a Michael Jordan. A sports great like

Jim Brown, member of the Football Hall of Fame, acknowledged that few could ever reach such athletic success, "Michael Jordan is a freak of nature—he's one of a kind." In fact,
a study conducted by Richard Lapchick at the Center for
Study of Sport in Society, showed that only about 1 in 12,000
black high school players ever make it to the pros in basketball. The other 11,999 are discarded at various levels from the
neighborhood playground, through high school and college.
Other findings are equally discouraging as an athlete looks to
the future. Louis Barbash found that less than half the football and basketball players on scholarships will graduate from
college. His research discovered that college players aspiring
to the pros face 400-1 odds. For those who make it, the chances
of staying are not good. The average career of a pro player is
six years, with most lasting only two. Why, then, does the
high school player pursue a grueling schedule of demanding
physical punishment when the odds are against him? Because
society and many high schools make it easier for the athlete
to thrive than the regular non-sports student.

Athletes often lead more pampered lives than other young
people. "A safety net goes out for athletes at an early age,"
said Clifford Adelman, a researcher for the U.S. Department
of Education who conducted an extensive survey of athletes
and academics. Murray Sperber in *College Sports, Inc.,* writes,
"Before 1986, the only NCAA rule on an athlete's college admission and eligibility for an athletic scholarship was a *C*
overall average in high school. Depending on the player's secondary education, the *C* average could be meaningful or not.
As former major league pitcher Jim Bouton says, 'Your outstanding jock has been on scholarship since the third grade,'
and has received special treatment from teachers and classmates along the way, most often the athlete's *C* average was
zero proof of his or her academic qualifications or aptitude for
higher education."

The sports obsession has crept, not only into the lives of
America's youth, but into high schools as well. Evidence of the
grandiose status given to sports in secondary school can be

seen in Permian High School in Odessa, Texas, where a $5.2 million football stadium was built for the Permian Tigers. Seating 20,000 fans, the stadium represents the inflated value the small town of Odessa awards its high school sports program. H.G. Bissinger in *Friday Night Lights* cites a budget for football medical supplies that exceeded the amount of money spent on supplies for the English department during one school year at Permian High School. In a northeastern high school the community raised a large sum of money to provide the football field with lights so night games could be played, yet the school newspaper had to postpone publication because it did not have sufficient funds to pay printing costs. When the community and school value sports above all else, and pay a high price for it, the student soon realizes that participation in athletics is more important than academics.

Teenagers today are brainwashed to believe that a successful sports career is not only feasible for them, but will be the answer to all their problems. Long term goals hold little appeal as they search for a way to be somebody on the high school campus. Philip Hoose argues, "Sports are over-emphasized, especially basketball and football, yet kids have to have something. It is not just that sports pulls them, it's the other side of the ledger, the incentive for studying, for accomplishing things, the joy of learning, that doesn't offer enough . . . the fun of it is gone. Compare it to what a Greek kid must have grown up with in the Hellenic period when knowledge was valued." Sports provide the young person with more enjoyment and glory than studying, as well as a disproportionate status among their peers that they have learned from society and the media is all important.

Athletics prevail over academics in the teenage perspective because of high visibility and quick rewards for effort expended. A teen craves popularity, admiration, or power in the tenuous high school social structure. The captain of the football team or the star basketball player possess this social omnipotence. Everybody admires or envies them. One teen summarized the situation when he said, "They get all the girls." Another senior thought a youth could get the same kind of status in other school activities, "But it comes much easier and faster in sports. The recognition brought through academics is not appealing to most people. Nobody in high school decides, 'Hey, I want to be a Nobel Prize winner.' It just doesn't work like that." Philip Hoose explained, "If you compare the glory that is available to the athlete with the glory that is available to the scholar, it just doesn't compare." The pressure to place athletics as a high priority is seen throughout the school and the students respond accordingly. Students and teachers both have bought into the sports mania and see their support and participation in the games as a totally positive force. Teachers, however, should know better, and refuse to participate in the glorification of an athlete at the expense of the majority of the students.

The tone set by the school is sometimes subtle, yet very effective in influencing the students' mindset. Scholars are listed on honor rolls, musical groups perform on stage in front of hundreds of people, poets and journalists are published, yet it is the athletes who are regularly paraded in front of the entire student body and introduced as individuals. The names and photographs of players appear constantly in school and local newspapers. Time is taken out of the educational day for pep assemblies and the students know why. Sports are important. One senior explained, "Getting introduced to the whole school at a pep assembly is really exciting. The school makes you even more of a star because of the emphasis it puts on sports." A glance into a typical classroom would not readily reveal the scholars present, but the highly visible athletes and cheerleaders would be easy to spot. On game days, athletes dress differently, in a jersey or a suit and tie, which sets them apart. Everybody knows they have a big game and lavish attention is paid to the competitors while non-team members are ignored. Morning announcements regale the school daily with the outcome of contests from the previous day. Richard

Lapchick said, "I think it is fine to honor and recognize the athlete, but the school has got to tell the student athlete that, just like the pros, he is a role model, he represents the school, and must be held to tough standards, *academically and morally*." Likewise, teachers have the obligation to make it clear to all students that athletes are expected to adhere to the same standards as the rest of the students and that favoritism will not exist.

Principal Ruby McClendon of Benjamin Mays High School in Atlanta, Georgia, stresses academics as the main event in her students' days and tells them, "You can be a good student and do other things, but you cannot do other things if you are not a good student." At her high school, an academic hall of fame exists as well as the traditional sports hall of fame. Students vie for admission to both, yet the academic awards won by the students far outnumber those awards for sports.

Unfortunately, the entire reputation of a high school can become directly linked to the athletic success or failure of its sports teams. Students have been conditioned to feel pride for a gifted sports school and embarrassment or even shame if their institution does not flourish on the playing field. Mrs. McClendon tells of helping a student keep athletic pursuits in perspective. "A student came to school one Monday and told me that someone at church had said that Ben Mays did not have a good football team. This bothered the young woman so I said, 'That's okay. We are just too busy learning our lessons.' "

She strives to make academics as exciting as athletics and says that in assemblies, "The students cheer for the academics as if they were an athletic event. We do not apologize for being an academic institution. We are proud of our athletes and they know it, but as far as we are concerned, everything else comes below academics on our priority list."

The game itself, however, creates a feeling that cannot be equaled by scholastics. One athlete felt schoolwork was important, but said, "Five thousand people are not going to go out to see a Nobel Prize winner on a Friday night with marching bands and pretty girls jumping around cheering for him." The excitement of the crowd and the game makes all the difference. Sports is an entertaining diversion from problems in life. The young man observed that books were also an entertaining diversion, but, "there are not thousands of other people out there reading with you." The thrill of the crowd attending a sports event is a great part of the lure. Joe Paterno, the extremely successful coach of Penn State football, agreed that the excitement of the game is like nothing else. He said, "I tell my players to enjoy it while it lasts. There is no other time when 85,000 people are going to stand up and cheer for you." But he also emphasizes the transient value of the notoriety gained from a successful sports career on any level. Paterno said he tells young athletes, "Get an education. Don't get sucked into a football or basketball mentality. When I talk to a kid when I am recruiting him, I tell him that ten years from now, when he is 27 or 28, three of his teammates might still be playing football. Probably none of them will. I ask, 'What is your life going to be like? What is going to replace the vacuum that is created by the absence of sports, all the effort, all the enthusiasm? Can you read and enjoy a book, give a speech, analyze problems? Can you run for political office? Will you be a good father? What are you going to do with your life? Are you going to be somebody that people respect, admire, look to for advice, look to for some leadership?

" 'Remember, you are someone who is in the forefront. You have been in the limelight. Everybody knows you, but they know you because you can bounce a basketball or run with the football. Someday they are not even going to know that you played football. What's going to happen then?' "

The school provides a different set of perks for the child of athletic ability. The American high school is a place where a youngster can win fame by kicking, running, shooting a basket, scoring a touchdown, wrestling, or hitting a baseball. When notoriety is available through the act of having fun, the student soon realizes that is the way to spend his time, not studying. The athlete does have to attend class as all other students do, but the incentive to study hard is often absent. The athlete learns quickly that he is special and certain considerations may be made for him. Richard Lapchick said, "The athlete realizes he is being treated in a special way. Maybe he gets dates more easily, or teachers give him a break, or maybe more people know him."

Teachers as well as students can become caught up in the exciting aura surrounding sports. Yet teachers have an obligation to hold fast in requiring athletes to make the grade as any non-athlete would . Sue Paterno, a volunteer English tutor for members of the Penn State University football team, spoke about the role of the teacher as well as the difficulties encountered when the teacher is confronted with a failing athlete during a sports season. She said the teacher must "Make sure the students know that the reason they are in high school is not to compete in an athletic event. They are in high school to get an education." She understands however, "If the teacher does not sign the eligibility slip that will allow that athlete to play he is going to have a set of parents mad at him, or have a coach mad at him." The route of least resistance would be to give the athlete a passing grade and avoid the pressure and problems resulting from the failing grade. However, the failing grade, if legitimate, must be given. "They [the parents or coach] will get over it. And somewhere along the line they will understand that the teacher is doing the best thing for their child. Why people can't know that . . . why it has to be a bitter confrontation is beyond me. I have seen parents get upset with Joe [Paterno] because he has kept kids out of competition because they have to upgrade their work in the classroom. They feel like, 'What are you doing to my son?' Trying to help your son, that's what he's trying to do. But it is hard to get that across."

Joe Paterno related an example of the type of athletic favoritism that happened at Penn State, but which also happens too often on the high school level as well. One evening Coach Paterno answered the telephone to find an upset graduate assistant teacher on the line. A Penn State football player taking his sociology class had apparently been cheating. When the teacher called Paterno, he felt he had a problem.

Paterno asked him, "What is the problem?"

He said, "Well, you know, he plays . . . and I don't know about the fans. I'd hate to flunk him."

Paterno countered, "What would you do if he weren't a player?"

The teacher replied, "Well, I'd flunk him."

"Then why wouldn't you flunk him now?" was Paterno's reply.

When the graduate assistant repeated his hesitation in failing the student and creating academic ineligibility because of his course, Paterno told him "Do you think you are doing him a favor by not flunking him? He knows what's going on. You have got to treat him like everybody else. That's part of the problem. The best thing you can do is flunk him. Call him in and tell him why you flunked him."

The player did receive a failing grade in the sociology class and when he approached Coach Paterno several days later, complaining about such treatment, Paterno said, "I'm glad he flunked you. I was afraid he wasn't going to."

Paterno vowed, "That's the attitude teachers have to take. If people think they are doing kids a favor because they are giving them grades, then they are just postponing the inevitable. All they are doing is seducing these kids into an attitude that because they are good athletes things are going to be taken care of. The other tragedy is that those kids [who are 'helped' by teachers] know they are not getting an education. They know they are not prepared. They have no confidence in themselves when they get out of school. They are lost souls and they know they have been cheated."

Dexter Manley, a former professional football player, courageously went public with an admission that he was unable to read despite a high school and college education. He related the disastrous effects of the routine special treatment he received from supposedly well-meaning classroom teachers. One high school Algebra teacher, who was also a coach, gave him a *B* in an algebra course in which Manley admits, "I didn't meet the standards." Manley, who had been enrolled in special education courses from second through seventh grade, knew he could not do the work, yet struggled to improve his academic skills. He said, "I used to go early to school for tutoring. There was a teacher who really worked with me at my junior high school. I felt so frustrated. There were times when I felt so insecure because I didn't know how to do it. It lowered my self-esteem, but eventually he 'gave' me a *B* anyway." He explained further about how rules conveniently changed for him, "Then I thought the rules didn't apply to me. Coaches helped me to cheat. They helped me pass." Because high school football in his home state of Texas led to public adoration and glory he felt little guilt in breaking the rules that governed less athletically gifted students. "I struggled in school. It was okay to cheat. It was okay to lie." Yet the breaks Manley was given were detrimental in the long run. He said that even though the deference of those in authority got him through school, "I felt like a cheat, like I'm no good." He did not learn to read or write in 12 years of school. All he was sure of was that, "It's okay to cheat as long as you don't get caught."

Astonishingly, the high school coach, according to Manley, ". . . knew that I couldn't read or write. He said you are never gonna make it. You're gonna get kicked out of college." Even more incredible was the fact that when Manley graduated from high school, he received 37 college scholarship offers, and admits that he could not even read a menu at a fast food burger joint. Dexter Manley eventually did escape a poor neighborhood and the corrupting influence of many of his peers through his participation in sports. He said, "I dreamed of being a football player. I was afraid that if I didn't have that dream that I would end up like the rest of my friends, doing drugs at an early age, and getting in trouble with the law." Unfortunately, in the end, the "rules do not apply" philosophy was too strongly ingrained and today Dexter Manley has been banned from the NFL for life after repeatedly failing to pass drug tests.

Joe Paterno writes in *Paterno: By The Book,* about the damage done to young people when schools fail to reinforce the proper academic expectations: "We have to make—and enforce—rules that enable us to get word to kids down through the high schools and through the elementary schools: If you have an ambition to be a college athlete but you don't want to study, you're not going to get into college. You're not going to be able to see yourself on television and say, 'Hi, Mom!' We have to use that carrot to get these kids to study—and to convince teachers that they owe these kids special personal attention. Everywhere I go recruiting, I find some teachers who assume that because a kid can bounce a basketball or catch a football and he can run with it, and because that kid isn't interested in studying, and because he comes from a family that doesn't own a book, and maybe he's black, that that kid is *ipso facto* dumb. In my experience, though, sometimes he's quick and smart as hell, but all the lessons of life have twisted his priorities out of whack."

Some teachers are simply blatant in their favoritism for athletes and create a situation in which the athlete is granted special favors while the rest of the class harbors resentment. One boy told of a teacher who, after spotting an exceptionally tall black student on the first day of class, observed to the students, "Looks like we have a basketball player here. I *love* basketball." The message was clear that the tall young man, who was indeed a basketball player, would be in line for some help during the season. During the semester, other students in the class felt that he was given extensions on his work, graded more leniently, and exempted from assignments because he had a difficult practice schedule or impending game. A student was not surprised by this, however, saying, "The athlete got the break . . . the athlete gets the break a lot of the time."

Even more instrumental than the teacher is the coach who can be the single, most important factor in the high school athlete's life. Sue Paterno pointed out, "High school coaches become almost fathers to some of the players and they have great dedication to their high school coach. They feel they owe them something and that is where the high school coach's influence can make the difference. A high school coach is a very influential person and can make or break a kid. If that high school coach stresses academics, the players on his team are sure to stress it as well. But if the student does not make up a test because the coach says he has to be on the practice field, then the coach breaks the kid. He has given the player the message that the classroom is not important.

"If the responsibility and the power that the coach has to influence the student is taken seriously, just think how that coach can urge an athlete to get good grades. Emphasis on studying has to come early, though, before high school. It always has to be academics first and athletics second." She explained, "Kids don't always understand the value of education; others must stress what the value is. The high school coach can be a powerful figure in selling the idea to his players."

Ron Bombick, chemistry teacher and coach at Bethesda-Chevy Chase High School in suburban Washington, DC, is "an academic teacher who happens to coach." Bombick agrees that the power of a coach is tremendous and maintains, "Coaching is also teaching. Kids have got to maintain their grades. If a teacher comes to me and says a player is doing poorly in class, I will tell that student that we must see an improvement or it will effect her playing time. Usually the grades improve. Sports can be a tremendous motivator, but the coach has got to put an emphasis on good grades. A coach has the responsibility to teach a kid priorities. If coaching is done right, you can give a young person a really positive experience that they can take into adulthood. Playing a sport gives a student a real sense of self. They can also take the discipline they learn playing a sport back into the classroom and when things get tough academically, they can draw on the sports experience and use the same determination they use on the field to overcome academic problems."

Bombick also feels being part of a team and accepting responsibility for adhering to a strict set of rules is an experience that will aid the young person in the future. He maintains that if they are not made to follow rules concerning academic eligibility they will begin to learn that they are responsible only for their own fate. "What they do as individuals impacts not only on themselves, but on the rest of the team that they are letting down if their grades are low. These are adult lessons to learn, but the athlete must learn them."

The academic standards in many school districts are shamefully low for high school athletes. Much-needed changes in requirements for athletic eligibility are being enacted across the country. The state of Texas is in the forefront of academic accountability for athletes. Following the 1983 publication of the report of the National Commission on Excellence in Education, *A Nation at Risk,* Texas Governor Mark White enacted a broad educational reform package. Most controversial was a no-pass, no-play provision for high school students, stipulating that no student would participate in any extracurricular activity unless a passing grade of at least 70 percent was received in every class. Any athlete who was ineligible under this rule would not play for a six week period until the next marking period's grades were distributed.

Coaches and parents strongly opposed the rule going so far as to fight the legislation in court. One of the major myths was that the less academically gifted students would not be able to attain the grades needed to play and would thus find other, less productive, pursuits. Parents of ineligible students went to court on the grounds that the ruling violated the Fourteenth Amendment rights of personal choice in family matters. They felt that they had the right to decide if the grades their children received were good enough to warrant membership on a team, not the state or the school. Following several different court cases, the Texas Supreme Court ruled that the legislation was Constitutional and provided great incentive for students to improve their academic performance in order to participate in extracurricular activities.

Much to the surprise of the opponents of the no-pass, no-play rule, academic performance by athletes did indeed improve. Richard Lapchick in *Pass to Play: Students Athletes and Academics* writes, "In Dallas, for example, the rate of ineligibility for varsity football players dropped from 16 percent in 1985 to 7.2 percent in 1986. For basketball, 11.8 percent were ineligible in 1986 compared with 17.8 percent in 1985. The results held true for the state. Texans expressed surprise. All the dire forecasts seemed unwarranted."

Similar scenarios have been played out across the country as jurisdictions attempt to raise the level of academic achievement needed for student-athletes. In 1982, Los Angeles city schools announced a similar *C* average requirement, with no failing grades allowed. Controversy inevitably followed as it had in Texas. During the first year of the new requirements, teams were hit hard as students became ineligible to play. By the second year, when all involved realized it was a serious regulation, the ineligible players met the new requirements and brought their grades back up to acceptable levels . El Toro High School serves as a good example of the results felt due to the changes. In *Pass to Play,* Lapchick writes, "Twelve football players were declared ineligible at the end of the first quarter. Without the players, El Toro lost in the second round of the conference playoffs. Don Walker, the principal, declared it a valuable lesson when all were eligible for the following year. As Walker told a *Los Angeles Times* reporter, 'We all respond to the two-by-four syndrome, and that was a two-by-four right across the head. The kids knew the requirements.

But no matter what we said they didn't listen until the grades came out. Then it hit them.'"

Coaches at El Toro helped greatly by monitoring grades and running required study halls for students in academic trouble. Walker said, "Coaches have a tremendous influence on kids. The policy has made kids much more aware through coaches. They really get on the kids and it's worked well. It's acted as motivation."

By 1989, however, only six states, Texas, California, Hawaii, Mississippi, New Mexico, and West Virginia, required at least a *C* average. Athletes around the country have proven that when the rules exist, and are strictly enforced, they will work hard in the classroom in order to be able to set foot on the playing field.

The delusion that a son or daughter will have great athletic success is counter-productive. A parents' time and encouragement is much better spent in promoting academic goals. The odds for almost all children are infinitely better that he or she can achieve academic rather than athletic success. It is more realistic to become a doctor than a professional quarterback. Some parents, however, unintentionally communicate the wrong values to their children, sometimes with the best of intentions. The support they show for a child's athletic endeavors may be misinterpreted if they are not balanced with interest and support for academics as well. Richard Lapchick said, "The parents send a subtle message that schoolwork is not as important when they only get involved with academics if the child is in danger of becoming ineligible. Those parents brag about being at every game the child has ever played, but do not show up at PTA meetings or on parents' night."

Parental pressure to excel in sports is probably the earliest influence in a child's life. Motives vary as a parent pushes sports for the youngster. A father of a current college quarterback bragged to the press that he always knew his son would make it big in football. In pursuit of this goal he said that he went so far as to have professional football coaches work with his son when he was 12 or 13 years old. Children cannot help but notice sports all around them, on television, on the school playground, in physical education classes. But most likely it is the parent who suggests the child join a team, sometimes as early as age four or five. One athlete recalled, "I've been in friends' houses where their dad is absolutely demanding sports. Some fathers will make their kids sign up for basketball camps, or they spend their whole summer involved in football. Everything is football, because the dad wants it that way." He understood the motivation, "Sure, everybody wants their kid to be the best, but the fact of the matter is that some kids are not."

Sue Paterno, said, "I worry about parents who are trying to live their lives through their kids, or trying to push the gifted athlete because he makes them look good." Many times, she said, "It is the parents who blame the coach for not playing the kid enough or benching him because grades are not up to par. All this does is teach the child that he does not need to take responsibility for his actions. It is always somebody else's fault."

Richard Lapchick also writes about parental favoritism. This coddling of athletes often begins at an early age when parents first note an affinity in a child for a certain sport. At that point the athletic child may be favored over other siblings in unobtrusive ways. Maybe the soccer player is exempted from taking out the trash because he has a practice or game. Perhaps he is given more help with his homework because of his busy schedule. He soon learns, however, that he is special, and his physical talents can provide him with benefits. These special incentives are then expanded to the school setting and the youngster who might have turned to academics soon sees that the more exciting route to acceptance is that of the playing field.

Psychological pressure placed on youngsters to achieve on the playing field can be devastating whether they make the team or not. Those who find that they are not good enough to play a sport competitively feel inadequate. One boy said, "It destroys your self-esteem and confidence if you don't make it. You feel you are not as good as somebody else."

Mental concentration is necessary for successful participation on a team, and when a high school student's focus is solely on sports, that young person cannot focus on the main business of high school: education and an adequate academic preparation for post-high school life. Advocates of high school athletics cite examples of kids who stay in school just so they can play. Although the athlete may be physically present, one wrestler points out that little if any learning takes place on the day of a competition. He said, "You are not thinking about school. You don't even want to be bothered about school. You are just there that day because you have to be in order to wrestle. You couldn't care less about anything else except that match because your mind is totally on that match you are going to compete in that night. Sometimes you don't sleep the night before because of nerves, so you are tired. Nothing sinks in during class."

The benefits of a young person's participation in sports cannot be discounted, however. One mother of a boy who had engaged in various sports explains the assets of a sports background, if athletics are not over-emphasized. She said, "My son was a fan of sports who focused on being a member of the team. It was clear he was not going to be a star, but he would be able to play and have small triumphs. He seemed to accept that. . . . Sports taught him discipline, responsibility to others, endurance of pain, acceptance of defeat, and pride in being part of something. He gained the awareness that he liked some boys and not others, but they were working toward something together. . . . As he grew older he made lasting friendships, learned to discipline his time and his body, all through good coaching, and encouragement from home, without undue pressure. . . . He was more disciplined while 'in training'. He ate well, slept well and knew that he had to keep the lessons up to date to be eligible to play in high school. He learned from experiencing an all-losing season at football. He got joy from a good play and learned to accept defeat as not being the end of the world, but a stepping stone to eventual success. He probably learned more from defeat than from victory. It is easy to win. To this day he cherishes memories of being part of the team."

For some high school students, sports programs enable them to better themselves as long as they maintain a good academic record. Successful participation on a team can teach discipline and sportsmanship. Some good students find themselves faced with a broader range of college choices if they have played several years of a varsity sport. Some students who are less academically inclined say their grades are better during a sports season because they know they have to pass to play. Others feel that if they were not on a team they would be "just hanging out and getting in trouble." For some, athletic talent guarantees entrance to college and escape from a bad home or neighborhood situation. Sports help create school spirit and pride that can tie a student body together. A team also provides a ready-made peer group and creates immediate social acceptance for a young person.

Without academics to back up the sports experience, however, the student is merely enjoying temporary benefits. When the games end, as they do for the vast majority of high school athletes, young people must be prepared academically and intellectually for the rest of their lives. The school must not fail in its duty to provide students with the proper training to succeed off the field, so that when they leave the games behind they may become competent and productive adults.

Saying Yes to
Drugs and Alcohol

"Parents are scared. They want to please their kids and make
them happy so they are afraid to 'just say no'."

JENNY BASTRESS
STUDENT

MANY AMERICANS MAY BELIEVE that the illicit use of drugs and
alcohol by adolescents is a problem well on the way to being
solved. Most would cite examples of rampant abuse in the
distant 60's and point out that the number of students showing up in high school classrooms under the influence of controlled substances has diminished greatly. They would say
that the classroom of the 90's is one that is free of substance
abuse and that educators should pursue other, more pressing,
problems as they attempt to teach teenagers in their charge.
Commonly considered an urban phenomena, primarily pla-
guing youth in metropolitan areas, the abuse of drugs and
alcohol remains one of the significant obstacles to learning for
all American teenagers. The presumption that only inner-city
schools need worry about teens involved in illegal activity, is
a tragically incorrect and naive assumption.

Although the habits of teens have changed somewhat in
past years, drug and alcohol use and abuse pose as great a

threat as ever in schools throughout the country. Young people can be found using drugs and alcohol regularly, in a variety of situations; before and during school hours, at parties, dances, and even before they engage in sporting events. Dealing with the use and acquisition of such substances interferes greatly with the education of today's youth. Sadly, the complacent attitude that parents, teachers and administrators have adopted in the wake of national anti-drug campaigns is part of the problem itself. Everyone thinks the problem has been taken care of by someone else and meanwhile, although much more subtly and subversively than in past years, the marketing and use of drugs and alcohol is flourishing among today's young people. Teens are constantly confronted in the schools with the temptation and availability to indulge in activity that can endanger their lives. The strength and potency of drugs available to the young person today greatly exceed the strength of substances in the past. Teachers, as they attempt to concentrate on teaching America's youth, are dealing daily with students who are preoccupied with buying, selling, or using drugs and alcohol, or more hopefully, avoiding peer pressure to do so. Students who abstain from substance abuse may fear attending school because they are confronted by peers urging them to buy and use. Social pressure to be part of the crowd can be devastating and a student worried about such weighty issues is harmed, as well as the student who abuses. Until the illicit use of drugs and alcohol is acknowledged as still being a significant threat, schools will continue to have an extremely difficult time in doing their jobs. Americans cannot be lulled into believing that the job of prevention has been done when, in fact, it has only begun.

During the past decade, millions of federal tax dollars have been spent on television public service announcements aimed at curbing drug usage among America's teenagers. These commercials, often featuring popular rock stars and entertainment celebrities, universally warn of the health risks of prolonged drug use and the dangers of drinking and driving. Still, despite these admirable efforts, both illicit narcotics and alcohol continue to plague the public schools and interfere with the process of education. A recent government survey determined that 51 percent, or some 10.6 million, secondary school students, grades 7 through 12, drink alcoholic beverages. Many young people claim to use liquor and beer to relieve boredom, escape stress, or simply to get high. They have little concern about the potentially adverse health consequences from such abuse or the dangers of drinking and driving. In 1989, over 2,800 teenagers died in alcohol-related automobile accidents, their deaths somberly memorialized in hundreds of high school yearbooks around the nation. Illegal drugs remain commonplace in most schools, although there appears to be an encouraging decline in their popularity. Still, over 50 percent of high school seniors admit to having used marijuana within the past year and acknowledge that such narcotics can be easily purchased in most public schools.

The use of such mood-altering substances continue to pose major problems for educators. Students who routinely use drugs and alcohol tend to lack motivation and a basic desire to learn. They frequently pose severe discipline problems since many attend school only for its social aspects. For them, academic classes are a mere nuisance which must be endured so they can meet with their friends, make important contacts, and learn when the next party will occur. According to Principal Jay Headman of Julius West Intermediate School in Rockville, Maryland, and founder of the Community Organization Against Drugs and Alcohol (COADA), "a lot of teens and families are having difficulty with their schooling because that is not the main importance. Just survival, just making it through the day is all that is important. . . . All people in education have to get the attention of a student before they can teach them anything . . . but some children in school are not tuned in because they have other things they need to deal with. Some drank too much the night before, some are dealing with parent arguments because one of the members of the family had been drunk, some are using drugs throughout the day. Education simply is not important to them . . . for they were using [drugs and alcohol] on a daily basis while others were using on weekends."

One high school chemistry teacher echoed the idea that students under the influence of drugs or alcohol could not be reached, but stressed that, even more importantly, they posed a physical threat in the classroom. "Teaching chemistry is difficult enough when all things are going right. But when I have students who have been drinking or smoking marijuana before they come to class it can be dangerous. They don't pay attention to instructions, they break equipment during labs and they are sometimes dealing with dangerous chemicals. You can't teach them when they are high. They are a danger to other students in my chemistry class and they are a danger to themselves."

The ease with which a young person can obtain alcohol or drugs is one of the main factors contributing to the problems teenagers face. For the vast majority, alcohol is the drug of choice since its use is widely accepted by society and denied to them only because of their young age. Glib television advertisements constantly extol the glamour of drinking by featuring beautiful women and handsome men in exotic settings, playing volleyball on the beach, and living "the high life". Surgeon General Antonia Novello reported, "[Students] said that ads made drinking look glamorous and fun. Specifically, they mentioned that the ads had sexy people in them: They mention things like: 'makes you look like you're accepted'— and that 'girls in the ads are skinny and I want to be like that.' Also, more than half the students knew that Spuds Mackensie was not the Coors mascot but the Bud Lite mascot—a fact that tells me these ads may be a stronger influence on students than they realize." According to Dr. Thomas Radecki, Chairman of the National Coalition on Television Violence, a child will see alcohol consumed on television over 75,000 times before reaching the age of 18.

Beer and wine manufacturers have made a calculated effort to appeal to the large youth market by producing a wide variety of sweet drinks such as wine coolers that make alcohol more palatable to teenage tastes. A survey entitled "Youth and Alcohol" revealed that secondary school students, all illegal drinkers, consume 1.1 billion cans of beer each year and over 31 million gallons of wine coolers. Furthermore, few students ever drink in moderation. At parties and other teen gatherings, drinking games are popular, with losers "forced" to consume large amounts of alcohol. Others are encouraged to "shot-gun" beer or use so-called "beer bongs" that enable teenagers to poor enormous quantities of booze directly down their throats frequently to the cheers of onlookers. Such binge drinkers, according to Novello, ". . . average more than 13 beers a week. In all, these young alcoholics drink 15 drinks a week. Some students drink as many as 33 beers a week, a dozen wine coolers, 24 glasses of wine, or 24 shots of liquor. Consuming these average amounts of beer, wine coolers, wine or booze, would cost a teenager more than they earn on part-time jobs!"

Many teens are easily able to afford these weekend parties due to inventive and prolific marketing practices on the part of party-givers and the generosity of older friends or even parents. A keg party may be advertised by word of mouth or flyers distributed surreptitiously at school. For about three to five dollars per person, a young person can purchase admission to a party, paying less at the door than they would to attend a movie or buy a pizza. Many times, money for the weekend blasts comes from unknowing parents who believe that they are paying for an innocent and legal pastime as they dole out ten or twenty dollars for their children's entertainment. Older friends sometimes foot the bill, but even if the teen is forced to buy his own alcohol, he finds the system that requires him to be of a certain age to drink can be shamefully lenient if he knows the right places to shop. Such establishments usually persist in ignoring the law until a complaint is filed by a concerned citizen with the appropriate alcohol control board, or local police. Surgeon General Novello observed, "Seven million of the students who drink, buy their own beverages. Even 12 and 13 year olds have told us they can easily purchase them! Teenagers use fake IDs, buy from stores that easily sell to them, or from stores that have young clerks. In Pennsylvania, where alcohol sales are controlled, the study showed that teens buy at houses called 'speakeasies' which sell to underage teenagers."

By far the most popular place for students to obtain and use alcohol is at private parties. Some may say that these do not encroach into the school day to generate difficulties, but they do. Preparations for, and speculation about, the weekend festivities permeate the already fragile concentration of students and further distract them from the educational tasks at hand. Private parties are generally held at a student's home when his parents are away for the weekend or just the evening. Parties also occur during the day when unsuspecting parents are both at work confident that their high school student is in class. One student noted, "If you wanted to, you could go to a party every night, every weekend." These gatherings range from a small group of close friends to massive school-wide affairs attended by literally hundreds of thirsty students. In some cases, elaborate maps and detailed lists of directions will be drawn up and covertly distributed to students at school. The potential for problems increases dramatically with the number of students attending a party. One individual remembered, "If you are having a party and you let it be known you are having a party, people are going to come that you aren't going to know and maybe that you don't like. There are a lot of fights at parties . . . [In one case] this boy was really drunk and he picked up a fire poker and was going to beat up this guy because he had received a rejection from a college that the other boy had been accecpted by. It took five of his friends to stop him."

One daytime party virtually disrupted an entire school as many students maneuvered between party and classes while others spent most of that Friday speculating about what was taking place at a "kegger" conveniently located right across the street from the high school. Shortly after both parents had left for work, older friends of the teenage hostess delivered several kegs of beer while, simultaneously, word went out that a party was in progress. Some students consumed numerous drinks at the young woman's house and then returned to school grounds, attending classes to visit friends and brag about their bold behavior. Drunken teens drifted into classes, disrupting the school day as they recruited peers to return to the party with them. Assistant principals and security guards shuttled back and forth between party and school, catching those who were too intoxicated to evade them and then calling parents to pick up the offenders. One young man, suspected of using much more than beer to get high, entered school and injured himself badly. Three teachers cared for him as they awaited the ambulance's arrival when they should have been addressing scholastic concerns. The following week the administration spent virtually all their time dealing with miscreants, holding parent conferences and supervising partygoers who had drawn in-school suspension as their punishment. Situations like this one are all too common.

A large number of students, coupled with heavy drinking, is a volatile combination. While some become violent, others seem to lose all sense of judgement and cause massive property damage. At one keg party, a student remembered, ". . . the house was so trashed. They had a massive food fight and people spilled stuff all over the carpets. When they had their parties there were so many people in the house it was impossible to control." Still, according to one girl, the litmus test of a truly successful party was "based on how much alcohol there was, how many people got drunk, and if weird things happened . . . The parties that were talked about were the ones that were out of control."

The most immediate and lasting consequence of teen drinking is the high death rate among adolescents caused by alcohol-related automobile accidents. Indeed, in large high schools, a student will be killed in such a tragedy virtually every year. Most schools have responded by forming local chapters of Students Against Drunk Driving (SADD). These student-run organizations attempt to raise the consciousness of the student body concerning the dangers of drinking and driving by mounting school-wide publicity campaigns. Red ribbons for automobile radio antennas are distributed throughout the community to display support for their efforts and students are given cards with special telephone numbers to call for safe, free rides home if they have been drinking. Before major school events such as homecoming, prom, and graduation, assemblies are conducted where students view graphic film footage showing the often fatal consequences of drinking and driving. Cars totalled in disastrous alcohol-related accidents are exhibited in front of the school and special guest speakers often tell students about their own personal stories and how their lives have been ruined by their failure to heed such warnings.

The sincere and admirable efforts of SADD coupled with the increase in the drinking age has apparently had some positive effect. The overall fatality rate among young drivers has, in fact, substantively declined since 1980 and more students profess to be aware of the need to have so-called designated drivers. But in an effort to remain credible with teenagers, SADD preaches only *no* drinking and driving but does not urge abstinence from alcohol altogether. Student SADD leaders tend to justify this seeming inconsistency on the grounds that students are going to drink anyway and that to urge them to do otherwise would only hurt their more important cause of reducing vehicular homicide. Most high school students, thus, feel unconstrained and continue to drink freely. Their sense of youthful immortality even allows them to redefine designated drivers as students who have had only three or four beers versus the more traditional ten.

One might think that teen drug and alcohol use does not infringe on the school day and the educational process if it does not take place on school premises or during the school day. What they do on their own time is the concern of the parents. Faculties of most schools, however, find themselves dealing regularly with such concerns. Much of the education that goes on in the adolescent years is socialization learned through events such as dances, sports events, and field trips. One of the most common anxieties of the teacher in charge of extracurricular activities is the contingency plan for students caught breaking rules and indulging in illicit activity as soon as they are outside of the confines and restrictions of parental influences. School officials obviously do not condone student drinking but students still partake frequently during school hours as well. Some students hide alcohol in their lockers or drink during lunch, careful to chew aromatic gum, like Big Red, to mask the incriminating smell.

Many of the extracurricular activities that regularly punctuate the school year offer ample opportunity for students to abuse alcohol. Some drink at football and basketball games, carefully disguising the fact by carrying large soda cups or cans filled with spiked drinks. During school-sponsored dances, small groups of students gather in the parking lot to socialize and drink, away from the scrutiny of teacher chaperons. The only evidence of such activity is the large number of beer cans and wine bottles that litter the school grounds the following morning.

One teacher felt that drinking at school dances was a severe problem. He said, "The fact that students will arrive at a dance drunk or high is a big fear I have. I hate to chaperon dances because we know the kids are going to show up high or drunk. In the classroom the teacher has more of a hold over them, but at a dance the students feel that we just don't have that much control." He felt that the problem was prevalent across the country. "The drug of choice may change, but the behavior doesn't change."

Some schools have opted for cancellation of school dances and other activities as they feel impotent in stemming the tide of student drinkers. Schools have no option other than removing the setting in which the abuse can take place. Regrettably, those drug- or alcohol-free students who behave properly and truly enjoy the activities are penalized, as they are deprived of a meaningful part of their high school experience. The abusers simply move to a different locale to pursue their partying unconcerned that they have ruined something valuable and irretrievable for others. Drinkers can drink all through their lifetime, but the time available for high school dances or activities is finite and cannot be recaptured.

Ironically, one of the worst nights for such excess is the prom. Once a night of special memories and magical moments for many students, today the dance is only an evening of blurred impressions. Indeed, drinking has become the focal point of prom night for far too many students. Parents often contribute to the problem by allowing their children to rent limousines for the occasion. This is justified on the practical grounds that it is a safe means of transportation on a night when many people will be drinking and driving, but many chauffeurs gladly provide students with ample amounts of beer, wine, and champagne for an extra fee. After dinner at a restaurant where students are often served liquor despite formal attire that clearly identifies them as underage promgoers, the students finally arrive at the dance. Since many high schools now hold such affairs in hotels, the students take advantage of this situation by renting rooms and suites. There they can retreat from the dance free from the scrutiny of teachers to imbibe further. The rooms also provide privacy and an intimate setting.

Far too many parents are grossly unaware of what their children are doing during their spare time. Indeed, many unknowingly are providing them with sufficient opportunity to drink. One astute student observed, "Parents don't have a clue to what is really going on. They don't want their child to be mad at them. They don't want to put their foot down and be the 'evil' parent so it's much easier to say yes." Another girl commented, "I think parents need to take a lot more responsibility. I mean the fact that kids use drugs and kids drink and stay out late, they don't learn that at school." The school, however, is the entity required to deal with the ramifications of such activities, in many respects acting as parents because mothers and fathers have abdicated their obligation to guide their own children.

Yet even those parents who profess to be aware of the situation do little to stop it. "The 60's children are the parents of today's children," one girl said. "They are still trying to say 'Do whatever you want but let's talk about it.' " Such parents often see teen drinking as a lesser evil than the harmful effects of drug abuse. According to Jay Headman, such attitudes are naive, "When [parents] look at it that way, you can be glad they are not into heavy drugs, but the number one killer of teenagers is alcohol. Abuse of alcohol can lead to suicide, unwanted pregnancies, AIDS, fights, violence, and car accidents. Alcohol is related directly to all those things. Parents need to know that and realize that it is illegal for teenagers to drink and it can have a tremendous impact on their child. Parent need their awareness raised."

While alcohol usage among teenagers remains high, the use of marijuana and other narcotics by students has been declining. A recent study conducted by the University of Michigan credited this encouraging news to a growing awareness among young people of the dangers inherent with drug usage. Despite this growing awareness of the damaging effects of drugs, youthful experimentation has not been deterred. Over 50 percent of high school seniors used marijuana during their final year of high school and one-third of those have at least tried harder narcotics.

The increased attention to the evils of drugs unfortunately has not inhibited the ready availability of such items in the typical high school. Students at affluent suburban schools can claim, "If I wanted to, I know who to buy drugs from." Indeed, in most schools, there remains a small cartel of students who continue to extol the benefits of drugs as a means to euphoria and who have little interest in anything else. For the most part, student drug abusers lack motivation, are subject to massive mood swings, and see their grades drop. Their primary motivation is to get high. One parent whose son got heavily involved in drugs during his freshman year wrote, "[going to school] was like going to drug camp every day. Back then, everything was so available. He began cutting classes, a common tip-off, but we didn't hear from the school until he was flunking everything. It turned out he was going to school for the first period, getting checked in, then leaving and smoking marijuana all day."

Federal drug enforcement officials uncovered one high school in which an astonishingly small ring of students sold an estimated 100,00 hits of LSD during a single year. Those individuals distributing and selling the drug were high school students catering to a clientele of mostly high school classmates.

Many students express nervousness at attending high school because of the prevalence and availability of drugs. Innocents are fearful of being approached by student salesmen or users and have no experience or skill in dealing with such situations. Some avoid extracurricular events in which they suspect illegal activities will take place. The law-abiding student is then the one punished as he excludes himself from activities meant for the majority of the school population while the law-breaker enjoys those perks.

Even though the good news is that fewer teens are using illegal drugs, the frightening fact remains that the drugs these students are using are more lethal than ever. Calvin Chatlos, M.D., writes in *Crack: What You Should Know About the Cocaine Epidemic*, ". . . every drug sold on the streets today is far more potent than ever before. Peter Bensinger, former head of the Drug Enforcement Agency, says that the difference between drugs of today and those of just a few years ago is 'like the difference between a bicycle and a Sherman tank.' "

Crack, a highly concentrated form of cocaine, is named after the sound the small rocks, resembling rock salt, make when they are burned and smoked. More powerful than cocaine, crack differs in that it is smoked rather than sniffed which increases the immediacy of its effect on the user. As the drug goes almost instantly from the lungs to the brain, the user experiences a high that comes less than twenty seconds after smoking, as opposed to a cocaine high which is felt anywhere from two to fifteen minutes later. The intense euphoria resulting from crack lasts about fifteen minutes and costs an seemingly affordable ten to twenty dollars for a vial of three or four small rocks. Its immediate and intensely pleasurable feeling, its availability, and affordable price all make crack appealing to the teenager.

Adolescents may not set out intentionally to try one of the harder drugs such as crack or cocaine, yet may do so if they are already intoxicated from alcohol or marijuana use. The diminished judgement of an intoxicated teen may lead them to throw caution to the wind and try crack just once "to see what it feels like." Experts and addicts agree that crack is not a drug that can be dabbled in for experimental purposes. Unlike other drugs that can be used without addicting the user, crack's power takes effect so quickly that the stage of casual usage is bypassed and the teen quickly becomes addicted.

LSD (lysergic acid diethylamide) is a drug which is regaining popularity recently after a steady decline following its heyday in the 60's. A hallucinogenic drug, LSD, commonly known also as acid, is colorless and tasteless and can be found as powder, a capsule, soaked on blotter paper, or as a clear liquid, sometimes dropped on sugar cubes. Extremely affordable, at three to five dollars a hit, LSD is readily accessible to teens. One boy said the place to get acid was "your local drug dealer." He said it was easily transportable because, in blotter form, it was small and could be slipped inside a notebook or textbook and it could be passed easily during a drug transaction since it looked like a sheet of paper. Other students have been known to surreptitiously hide small amounts of acid on blotter paper inside the cellophane wrapper of a cigarette pack where it can closely resemble the state seal that usually appears there. Although LSD does not have a high dependency or tolerance potential and is not considered particularly addicting, the negative effects of a bad experience with the drug, a "bad trip," can be psychologically damaging and lead to psychosis or even suicide.

High school students who use LSD sometimes take the drug before attending a concert hoping that the action of the drug, blending with the sensory impressions of the music will result in an enhanced appreciation of the performance. Some save acid as a drug to do for other special occasions. One recent graduate cited the example of doing acid for the Fourth of July. "We knew we were going to the Mall (in Washington, D.C.) for the celebration, and we wanted to heighten the experience by doing acid. With the fireworks and the amazing visuals and all the people in the crowd, we thought it would be great." Some see LSD as a learning, mind-expanding experience and drop acid to see a different dimension to life, much like the followers of Timothy Leary in the 60's. Since each acid trip is different according to the environment and mood of the user, some young people repeatedly use it to see what they may discover with each consecutive usage. Others report taking LSD as a remedy for boredom. With an uneventful day before them, they see a trip as a way of doing something different or thrilling. One young man said, "Acid is definitely a thrill-seekers drug. Some people even take LSD and go skiing so the feeling is heightened as they fly down the slope. Because it is a very functional drug, it keeps you up and going, it is fun to do for a special event."

One of the most disastrous aspects of LSD usage is that the novice teenage user may not realize the capricious nature of the drug. Since the effect of the drug can be different each time it is taken, no guarantee exists that a user will not have a bad experience. One young man said, "The really bad thing about LSD is that it lasts eight to twelve hours and there is no getting off once you have gotten on. If you are having a bad time, you know that it won't end for a long time. You're stuck."

Marijuana, the most commonly used illegal drug today, is the drug often seen as a "gateway drug" that leads to the use of other drugs. Yet, many teenagers regard "pot" as a harmless part of the adolescent scene. Young people rarely make the choice to try a drug like crack or LSD for their first encounter with drugs. They almost universally begin with marijuana. Some see no problem at all with the drug and vow it is no different than having a beer. Robert L. DuPont, Jr., M.D. writes in *Getting Tough On Gateway Drugs*, "One of the disastrous drug myths is that marijuana is a 'soft' and therefore unimportant drug." Most drug users and abusers started with alcohol and marijuana and then went on to harder drugs.

Young people use marijuana for various reasons ranging from a desire to experience altered sensory perception to wanted to relax or "kick back." One boy said it was a "mellow feeling" and calmed him down. The initial high from smoking the drug lasts two to four hours but the harm that even temporary marijuana use can do to a teen can be lasting, stunting emotional growth and inhibiting learning.

Schools have to deal with the results of drug use and abuse on a daily basis. When drug or alcohol abuse is detected, it is most often dealt with strongly. The difficulty exists, however, when teachers do not detect the use of drugs on the part of the students. Many times, this is not through intentional neglect by school personnel, but because of an ignorance of the symptoms of drug and alcohol use and hesitation to take a chance of wrongly accusing a child of abuse. Education can enable teachers to know the signs of an intoxicated teen so that they can confidently take action to get a young person into treatment.

One such educational session, with a local policeman displaying actual samples of the array of drugs available on the street, left most of a high school faculty highly enlightened as they had no previous knowledge of the subject. One teacher was so unacquainted with the drug culture that when students fashioned pottery bongs for smoking marijuana in her art class, she had no idea what they were. Others commented that they thought certain students found sleeping in class, who were known abusers, were only fatigued and not under the influence of drugs. When more teachers know what to look for in their students' behavior, the war on drugs can take another step as miscreants are caught and helped with their problems.

For many students, addiction is never going to be the obstacle standing in their way. They may, however, be harmed when they use or abuse drugs or alcohol and exercise poor judgement as a result of such use. All students must know the danger they face as they dabble in illegal substances. Some may be tragically injured or killed in an automobile accident, but harm can befall a student who uses poor judgement in other ways. A high school coach cited numerous examples, "Players sometimes come to practice after school acting uncoordinated when I know they are star athletes. I know that they have been doing something and they could get hurt on the playing field. I've had kids who showed up for night games who have had a couple of drinks. One time a player arrived drunk after a 'Spirit Party.' I have also had other team members tell me that players are high or drunk and I should keep my eye on them."

Jay Headman said, "A lot of these kids never get addicted, but . . . the impact of temporary abuse will affect them for the rest of their life. Some of the kids will never be addicted to the drug, but will abuse it and abuse it consistently. We need to constantly go back to them and say that you made it this time but you are playing against the odds and the next time you might not be so lucky."

Most experimental drug use happens in the adolescent years. Robert L. DuPont, Jr. M.D. in *Getting Tough on Gateway Drugs,* writes, "To many Americans today, adolescence is a mess. When alcohol and drug use are added, the mess becomes deadly." During this turbulent time in a young person's life, adults figure prominently in guidance roles to help young people avoid the pitfalls. DuPont explains, "Too many parents have given their 12- to 18-year-olds too much responsibility for their own behavior. Too many teenagers are treated and expect to be treated by their parents as 'Pseudo-Adults' who have the rights and independence of adulthood, but without the responsibilities that go with that status.

"Rather than establish and enforce firm rules, some parents—when confronted by the desire to treat their dependent children as adults rather than children—hide behind the rationalization that 'children need to learn to be adults by making their *own* decisions.' This is a parental cop-out. Sure, kids need to learn to be adults by making their own decisions, but not by doing anything and everything they please. That is poor preparation for adulthood. Children need to learn to become adults by understanding, accepting, and working within reasonable rules for behavior, including participation in family life and avoidance of alcohol and other drug use. An intelligent parent does not teach a three-year-old about the dangers of crossing the street by 'letting her learn for herself,' any more than a parent of a 16-year-old about the dangers of drug use by 'letting him learn for himself.' "

As children pass through adolescence, activities to broaden them educationally, physically, emotionally, and spiritually are the pursuits that help form a successful adult. Drug and alcohol use by teens stunts growth in all of these areas, and teachers and parents must take an active role in guiding teenagers through the enticements from peers and the media to indulge in a lifestyle that can only harm them.

The intrusion of drugs and alcohol into the school day is distracting and disruptive as students are not focusing on the best investment for the future—an education. Instead, adolescents too often grab for the short-term gratification of enticing forbidden fruits. As they engage in activities that many a teen would be quick to declare is nobody's business but their own, they inadvertently affect countless others. The effect of drug and alcohol abuse on school programs, personnel and innocent students is pervasive and until it is eradicated, schools will not be able to concentrate fully on the academic preparation of America's young people.

Chapter
Eleven

Sensible Reforms
for Modern Schools

"Education made us what we are."

C.-A. HELVETIUS

WITH THE NEWS COMING FROM PUBLIC SCHOOLS mostly bad,
many in the United States have abandoned any real hope of
enacting realistic educational reform. With an increasingly
diverse student body and the constantly increasing demands
of a complex society, they have instead resigned themselves
to the current system which perpetuates mediocrity, frustrates academic ambitions, and denies far too many young
people a high-quality education. Teacher unions and other
critics of American education have simplistically reduced all
educational problems to a matter that more state and federal
money can miraculously solve. They argue for more programs,
reduced class size, and increased teacher salaries but ignore
many of the more fundamental problems faced by the schools
and are oblivious to the stark realities of governmental budgets in austere economic times.

The public schools, however, can be substantially improved
without large, new appropriations or tax increases and the
implementation of grandiose programs. What is needed first
is an honest and forthright assessment of the role of public

schools in American society followed by the re-allocation of existing financial resources. Parents, teachers, administrators, and students must form a solid partnership committed to improving academic requirements, offering challenging and interesting curricula, providing a safe and conducive educational setting, and establishing sound academic priorities. Only then, will the United States see progress toward transforming public schools into centers of learning.

1. School-based Management. Over the past several years, large, entrenched educational bureaucracies have centralized the decision-making process for public schools and have seized control over virtually all major educational policies. Crucial financial decisions and funding appropriations are entrusted to people who have absolutely no educational training or classroom experience and who are, in fact, more comfortable with ledgers than with children. The end result is an educational establishment which is more efficient at balancing budgets than implementing programs. It is an establishment that continually fails to address the important needs of students. The modern educational bureaucracy conspires to thwart efficiency by generating massive amounts of red tape which effectively frustrates teachers and principals alike. The most important and immediate educational reform that can be implemented during the next decade is to eliminate bureaucratic inefficiency by adopting an effective system of school-based management, one that empowers principals, teachers, parents, and students and entrusts them to run the day-to-day operations of the school.

Schools which are separated only by a few miles, even within the same jurisdiction, can have widely differing student populations and face vastly different problems. The individual high school principal, as the senior on-site manager, is the person most capable of assessing the important needs of the school and of developing effective programs to address them. School boards must trust their high school principals by granting them the power to run their schools, free from undue bureaucratic interference and with the mandate to improve the quality of education for their students. This must include control of the school's annual operating budget since allotment of funds invariably sets a school's educational priorities. From this pool of money, the principal would be expected to determine what equipment needs to be purchased or replaced, which courses should be taught, what library books must be acquired, and which field trips to fund, all predicated upon the school's population and individual makeup.

An effective school-based management system virtually eliminates the need for large numbers of high priced out-of-school support personnel. They are replaced, instead, by committees of dedicated parents, committed teachers, and willing students who would be expected to contribute advice, offer expertise, and provide assistance to the school's administration. With the close and meaningful partnership of teachers, parents, and students established, the result would be an improved learning environment and a more efficient school.

2. Require Principals to Teach. The principal is the most important person to the overall success or failure of a school. Not only is the principal expected to be the school's chief administrator, he or she is also its educational leader. To reaffirm this commitment, all principals should be required to teach one class each semester. Assistant principals and other administrators would be expected to deal with any issues or problems that might arise during that one sacred period.

There are several advantages to principals returning to the classroom. First and foremost, it increases their daily contact with all students, not just the disruptive ones. This high profile presence and sense of accessibility is a common factor in the overall success of all good principals. Furthermore, it requires principals to live by their own rules and policies. In the classroom, responsibility for the same attendance procedures, forms, reports, grades, and other duties that they require of their staff provides a sense of reality that is otherwise missing. It also shows a strong sense of commitment to education and helps the faculty to perceive the principal as a colleague as well as a supervisor.

3. Preservation of the School Day. In the United States today, the average public school is open only 180 days for actual instruction, some 30 percent less than in Japan and Germany. It is remarkable that even more time is wasted with frivolous activities and other academic disruptions. To truly reform the American public schools, principals and administrators must be committed to making each school day a time of meaningful, purposeful instruction.

Assemblies and pep rallies should be offered only on special occasions and should not become routine. Students should be expected to be in class. Meetings with counselors, college visits, medical appointments, and other extracurricular activities should not ever interfere with instruction. Sporting events and club competitions must be scheduled only after school because when students miss class, that day's activity is forever missing from their academic background and such time is simply irreplaceable.

The last day of the school year should be used effectively by teachers to help prepare the students for their next year's courses. Since underclassmen have already completed their registration and know what subjects they will be taking, they should be sent to their new course instructors to be issued reading lists and homework assignments to complete during the summer holidays. This would ensure that their vacation is not void of learning and would establish the important expectation that when the students return to school in the fall, they will be ready to begin immediately with the academic program.

4. Eliminate Academic Tracking. Over the past several years, academic tracking has quietly returned. Weaker students are channeled into basic or skills courses which seldom challenge them or expect them to excel. They graduate doomed to a life of limited choices since they have little hope of ever attaining any academic excellence. The average students, likewise, are separated from their more gifted class-mates. These classes are characterized by a general sense of mediocrity with students lacking motivation, leadership, or desire. To help improve academic standards for *all* students, classes should be grouped heterogeneously with all students pursuing roughly the same core curriculum.

Teachers should emphasize cooperative learning in their classes. This methodology encourages peer instruction and a positive sense of working together to attain knowledge, with students sharing their information and research with others. Talented students should be expected to assist other students and provide quality role models to emulate. Most importantly, the negative stigma of basic and regular classes is removed and students are given more challenging and rewarding work. Heterogeneous classes place excellence as the standard rather than mediocrity, with all students expected to succeed.

5. Require Algebra. One of the most important challenges facing American education is the improvement of student performance in mathematics. A recent survey concluded that only 36 percent of high school seniors could solve even the most basic of equations, hardly surprising given the fact that American students can graduate having completed only the most rudimentary of mathematics courses. All high schools should mandate algebra as a prerequisite for graduation since this single course has had a significant correlation to improving student performance in other subject areas as well.

Algebra is considered to be a "gateway" class. It offers students a vast array of options since chemistry, physics, trigonometry, and calculus cannot be effectively studied without mastery of algebra. As importantly, it helps students develop thinking skills, logical reasoning, and self-confidence.

6. Hold students Accountable for Behavior. Adequate discipline is vital to a successful school environment since no one can effectively learn amidst chaos and disorder. Far too many public schools today encourage disruptive behavior by failing to impose consequences for inappropriate behavior.

A school must make its expectations clear to its student body by publishing and distributing its rules and regulations. Insubordination and disobedience should not be tolerated under any circumstances. When students violate the rules, there must be immediate and obvious consequences for the infractions. Punishment must be consistent and fair, so that students know the results of their behavior.

Suspension is necessary for continually disruptive students. In such cases, the parents must be inconvenienced by the administration in order to deal with the situation. A suspended student should only be allowed to return to school after a parent conference with an administrator and a guidance counselor to ensure that the parents are aware of the problem. Students who continually defy rules or refuse to modify their behavior, also must be dealt with. In extreme cases, the responsibility of the administration changes from trying to correct the behavior to protecting the student body from educational and emotional harm. It is their responsibility to build a paper trail, to chronicle and document the problem, to remove the offending student and grant alternative placement. No student has the right to interfere with the rights of others or to jeopardize their right to a quality education.

7. Establish a Firm No-Use Drug Policy. Drugs and alcohol have no place in American public schools and there should be absolutely no tolerance for such abuse. Health classes need to teach all students about the adverse health consequences associated with such use. Those students who are apprehended using drugs or alcohol during the school day should be suspended from school and required to undergo corrective counseling. This policy should be applied to all school-sponsored activities including sporting events, field trips, dances, and plays. Those students who bring drugs to school with the intent to sell or distribute should be expelled without exception.

The school's PTA must make drug and alcohol issues one of their major priorities. To help educate parents concerning the problem, regular seminars should be offered, especially those which explain the patterns of adolescent behavior that indicates potential addiction. Parents must also be sure that all teen parties and other large group activities are adequately chaperoned by adults. Lists of parents pledging to abide by these standards should be circulated by the PTA to the entire school along with telephone numbers so that an efficient school-wide network is established. Individually, parents must know where their child is going at night and should establish reasonable curfews which they enforce. To ensure compliance, they should stay up until their child arrives home. Likewise, they should look for any tell-tale signs of substance abuse. Ridding the schools of alcohol and drug abuse requires parental cooperation and support.

8. Increase Parental Involvement. Parents have a vital and irreplaceable role in a child's education. They must establish education as a clear priority in their household by providing a quality home environment that is conducive to learning. The first step in achieving this aim is to turn off the television and to establish a daily time period devoted exclusively to study, free from all interruptions including telephone calls. Even after a student has completed his homework, the remainder of the time should be devoted to reading or studying. Parents also need to check and monitor homework to ensure that it is completed properly. They should also discuss with their children their progress in their classes and what they are studying. When appropriate, outside excursions and weekend trips to museums, art galleries, or a historic site should be scheduled to supplement the child's classroom experience and to support the work of their teachers.

Close communication between parents and teachers is essential. There should be no hesitation by concerned parents to call the school to talk to a teacher or, if they have concerns about their child's progress, to schedule an after-school parent conference through the guidance department. If practical, parents can assist the schools by volunteering periodically to provide administrative assistance; calling other parents to check on absent students or chaperoning field trips and extracurricular activities. During test days, parents can even proctor examinations to free teachers to observe other faculty members' classes or to grade essays and other assignments. This high profile presence not only shows concern but would truly heighten the sense of the school being part of the community.

9. Use a Multicultural Approach. For generations, the American public schools operated in a homogeneous environment. The curriculum developed during that period reflected a white, Eurocentric prejudice and denied or even ignored the many contributions of minorities and ethnic groups to science, literature, and history. In recent years, the schools have gained an increased awareness of the failures of the past, but it is important that teachers adopt a truly multicultural curriculum, especially in English and Social Studies courses, which includes the contributions that minorities have made to American society.

History and literature cannot be studied in a vacuum. To adequately understand slavery, it is vital for students to understand the states' rights philosophy of John C. Calhoun but it is equally important for them to read Frederick Doulgass' powerful and eloquent slave narrative denouncing the institution. Likewise, westward expansion cannot be adequately studied without a detailed explanation of native-American culture nor should the 19th century be covered without learning about immigration. A curriculum of cultural inclusion does not mean abandoning scholarship for mere political expedience. Teachers must resist the pressure to include spurious claims and wild accusations put forth by so many special interest groups who have little concern about truth or accuracy. It is time, though, for high school teachers to fairly credit the contributions of all Americans so that the rich cultural legacy of the United States can be truly appreciated and comprehended.

10. Make Use of Technology. Educators need to be more willing to use existing technology in the classroom. Far too many teachers are afraid of new equipment and continue to use the same methods and materials they did when they began their careers, oblivious to the exciting innovations now available in most schools. Even those teachers willing to use computers often incorporate them in a way that reduces the equipment to little more than a glorified typewriter.

Teachers must keep current with advances in technology. In the past decade, an information revolution has occurred making unimaginable resources readily available. CD-ROM now offers entire encyclopedias and enormous data-bases on disk in an almost instantly retrievable format; computers can generate accurate student progress and grade reports in a matter of minutes with public domain software costing less than five dollars; laser disk technology allows teachers to design specially programmed lessons; and high quality videotapes are available for classroom use for less than twenty dollars. Despite these resources, only a handful of faculty members avail themselves of such exciting technology, which has enormous promise in motivating students. Inservice training should be required of all teachers to incorporate these advances into their classroom in order to improve their classes and simplify their record keeping.

11. Recognize Student Achievement. An ongoing program to recognize the special accomplishments and talents of all students should be established by all high school principals. By keeping effective channels of communication open with teachers, guidance counselors, and parents, a truly informed principal can routinely give appropriate credit to students for their personal and academic achievements. Even a simple note of acknowledgement or a special certificate of recognition can be a meaningful expression which would show all students that they are valued and appreciated members of the student population. Well-publicized honor rolls, academic halls of fame, bulletin boards highlighting student activities, and public address announcements should all be utilized in an effort to credit excellence and performance.

12. Monitor Student-Athletes' Academic Progress. During a sports season, student-athletes should be required to return a form signed by all of their teachers which lists the student's current grade, a conduct evaluation, and a brief comment on their progress. These reports should be used by the coaching staff to carefully monitor student athletes to ensure that they are adequately performing in their academic classes and to determine their eligibility. If a grade is not satisfactory or if a teacher indicates that a student's conduct has been inappropriate, he or she should be either benched or suspended from the team regardless of their playing ability or stature until significant improvement is noted. Such a policy would quickly send a message that a student's academic classes supersede their involvement in sports.

Furthermore, in competitive sports that require a major commitment of time such as football and basketball, coaches should be required to hold mandatory study halls for all student-athletes. During these periods, the students would be expected to complete all of their homework, read required books, and study for examinations before they are allowed to practice.

13. Dismiss Ineffective Teachers. Those teachers who are constantly ineffective or incompetent should not be tolerated in the nation's public schools. Principals and administrators need to quickly identify such teachers and immediately provide administrative support to help them improve their skills and classroom performance. Department chairmen should also intervene by regularly observing an ineffective teacher's classes, assisting them in the preparation of lesson plans, and by helping them devise effective teaching strategies. Deficient teachers should be given every opportunity to improve their skills and to modify their professional behavior, but if after a reasonable amount of time, they are incapable of effecting substantive change, they should be summarily dismissed from the teaching profession. Teaching is one of the few professions where an ineffectual person can inflict lasting harm upon large numbers of people and, as a result, incompetence should not and cannot be tolerated.

14. Offer a Regular Leave-of-Absence to Teachers. Teachers should have the opportunity to take a one year leave-of-absence without pay for every five years of accumulated service. The constant pressure of motivating 150 students each day, contending with mounds of paper work, and dealing with serious behavior problems is both frustrating and exhausting. A brief break, free from such stress, would serve to invigorate many educators and help reduce the serious problem of teacher burnout. To help teachers afford an unpaid leave, school systems should allow an educator to designate up to 10 percent of their annual salary for sabbatical leave. These funds would be kept in an interest bearing account and would be available to teachers during their leave period or at any other time with a slight penalty for withdrawal. In return, the system would merely guarantee that a teacher could return after a one-year absence without penalty or loss of seniority. It would thus cost a school system virtually nothing but the overall, positive impact would be to improve staff morale and would serve to preserve a large veteran teaching staff.

15. Involve Prospective Teachers in the School. Students who wish to pursue education as a career in college, should be required to volunteer in the public schools for a minimum of two hours per week as part of their course load. Paired with a veteran teacher, they would immediately benefit from practical, hands-on experience and an early exposure to the true realities of American public schools. They would also have the opportunity to regularly interact with high school students, to offer tutoring assistance, and to teach their own lessons under the guidance and supervision of a skilled professional. This would not only improve a prospective teacher's preparation, it would help them to effectively evaluate their career goals to determine whether or not they truly wish to teach.

16. Invite Teachers to Address College Education Classes. Universities and colleges should actively involve high school teachers in teaching training classes. Active high school teachers can discuss with college classes important topics dealing with teaching methods, subject matter, discipline, and offer their own insights. Prospective teachers would benefit from sound, sensible advice on proven teaching methodology and would learn how to prepare effective lessons that present complex subject matter in a manner understandable to adolescents.

17. Implement a Mentoring System for New Teachers. In today's schools, new teachers are thrown into the classroom with little support or encouragement. Teaching is one of the few professions where a novice is doing exactly the same job, with the same expectations, as a veteran employee. Often the teacher is assigned a room and a schedule, required to attend pre-school meetings and periodic faculty and department meetings, and then left alone to teach. The abrupt withdrawal of even the weak support system in place during college training can leave a novice reeling as they try to acclimate themselves to the school, colleagues, curriculum, students, administration, parents, paper work, extra duties, and endless minutia that goes on behind the scenes in today's schools.

Training America's teachers throughout their entire career must be a top priority. Top-notch, experienced, successful high school teachers must be utilized to continually train both new teachers as well as their colleagues, not only in pedagogy, but in survival skills that will aid effectiveness in the teachers' respective schools. Mentoring programs for first-year teachers are necessary so that school systems make good investments in the teachers who will be teaching for the next few decades. By nurturing the new professionals, the schools not only provide much needed support, but also help to shape the new teachers into contributing members of their faculties instead of allowing them to flounder and either sink or swim on their own. The period necessary for "breaking in" a new teacher is shortened considerably, yielding beneficial results for students, teachers and the school as a whole.

18. Improve Inservice Training. Inservice training for experienced teachers should be intellectually challenging and relevant to a teacher's content area. Emphasis should be given to providing educators with proven lesson plans and teaching strategies that can be immediately implemented in the classroom. During such meetings, time should be allotted to allow teachers to exchange ideas, to share their teaching experiences, and to discuss professional concerns.

Money for extensive inservice training involving high-priced consultants and out-of-school experts could be saved or re-allocated to bring the kind of training that teachers really want and need. The common cry of, "Save the theories, give me something I can use now," could be satisfied by the introduction of inservice sessions taught by school-based instructional leaders.

19. Alternative Certification in Key Subject Areas. To encourage professionals to make the transition to teaching in key subject areas such as science, math, and vocational education, standard certification requirements should be modified. A conditional certificate should be created which would allow mid-career changes. These new teachers could begin working in the schools after being paired with another faculty member at a reduced salary. At night and during the summer, they would be expected to complete the academic requirements for their credentials.

The American public schools have been mired in mediocrity for years, ignored except by people who use meaningless rhetoric to lament the conditions without offering any substantive reform. Lack of discipline, poor teacher morale, ineffectual principals, top-heavy bureaucracies, political zealots, apathetic students, and archaic teaching methods have each contributed their own portion to the current lamentable situation. Yet, excellence in public schools remains an attainable goal if parents, teachers, students, and community leaders insist upon realistic reform and proven values that demand quality. Public education remains the single most important resource for students to become productive, informed, and skilled adults. It is imperative that the nation as a whole commit to the common purpose of providing quality education for all students so that the public school's report card will reflect such a commitment to excellence. The students of America deserve no less.

Selected Bibliography

Adelman, Nancy. *An Exploratory Study of Teacher Alternative Certification and Retraining Programs.* Washington, D.C.: Policy Studies Associates, Inc., 1986.

Adelman, Nancy. Personal Interview. 23 September 1990.

The Age of Indifference. Times Mirror Center for the People & the Press. Press Release: 28 June 1990.

Aikens, Linda. Personal Interview. 29 June 1991.

Aikens, Shelby. Personal Interview. 29 June 1991.

Alter, Jonathan and Lydia Denworth. "A (Vague) Sense of History," *Time.* Fall/Winter Special Edition, 1990, pp. 31-33.

Appleton, Robert. Personal Interview. 23 July 1990.

Attacks on the Freedom to Learn. Washington, D.C.: The People for the American Way, 1990.

Avery, Catherine. "Finding Alternative Ways to be Teachers," *Washington Times.* 5 August 1991, pp. G-3, G-4.

Babington, Charles. " 'Minority' Labels in Montgomery Schools Attacked," *Washington Post.* 3 July 1991, pp. C-1.

Bachike, Jessie. Personal Interview. 29 April 1991.

Bastress, Frances. *Teachers in New Careers: Stories of Successful Transitions.* Cranston, Rhode Island: Carroll Press, 1984.

Bastress, Jenny. Personal Interview. 23 March 1991.

Bennett, William. *American Education: Making it Work.* Washington, D.C.: GPO, 1988.

Bennett, William. *Our Children & Our Country: Improving America's Schools & Affirming the Common Culture.* New York: Simon and Schuster, 1988.

Bennett, William. Personal Interview. 3 April 1991.

Bombick, Ron. Personal Interview. 25 August 1991.

Breakiron, Diane. Personal Interview. 27 August 1991.

Britt, David R. *The All-American Cocaine Story: An Insiders Guide to the Realities of Cocaine.* Santa Barbara: JDA Publishing, 1983.

Burwell, Hope. Personal Interview. 29 October 1990.

Butler, Carolina. Personal Interview. 29 April 1991.

Chatlos, Calvin. *Crack: What You Should Know About the Cocaine Epidemic.* New York: Perigree Books, 1987.

Cheney, Lynne V. *American Memory: A Report on the Humanities in the Nation's Public Schools.* Washington, D.C.: GPO, 1987.

Cheney, Lynne V., Chairman: The National Endowment for the Humanities. Telephone Interview. 12 Feb. 1991.

Cheney, Lynne V. *Tyrannical Machines: A Report on Educational Practices Gone Wrong and Our Best Hopes for Setting Them Right.* Washington, D.C.: GPO, 1990.

Citrino, Anna. Personal Interview. 29 Oct. 1990.

Colglazier, Cathy. Personal Interview. 17 January 1992.

The Condition of Teaching: A State-by-State Analysis, 1990. By the Carnegie Foundation for the Advancement of Teaching. Princeton: Princeton University Press, 1990.

Cooper, Kenneth J. "Algebra = Job Prospects?" *Washington Post.* 1 April 1991, pp. A-1, A-7.

Cutright, Melitta J. *The National PTA Talks to Parents: How to Get the Best Education for Your Child.* New York: Doubleday, 1989.

Department of Health and Human Services. *Youth and Alcohol: A National Survey Do They Know What They're Drinking?* Office of the Inspector General, Washington, D.C.: GPO, 1991.

Department of Health and Human Services. *Youth and Alcohol: A National Survey Drinking Habits, Access, Attitudes, and Knowledge.* Office of the Inspector General, Washington, D.C.: GPO, 1991.

Diegmueller, Karen. "At Union's Convention, 'Paradoxes' of Free Speech," *Education Week.* 31 July 1991, p. 15.

Dupont, Robert L. *Getting Tough on Gateway Drugs: A Guide for the Family.* Washington, D.C.: American Psychiatric Press, Inc., 1984.

Drew, Ann. Personal Interview. 30 April 1991.

Eastman, Alex. Personal Interview. 13 Feb. 1991.

Eikel, Bob. Personal Interview. 2 August 1990.

Elmore, Richard F. et al. *Restructuring Schools: The Next Generation of Educational Reform.* San Francisco: Jossey-Bass Publishers, 1990.

Engel, Joel. *Addicted: In Their Own Words: Kids Talking About Drugs.* New York, Tom Doherty Associates, 1988.

Escalante, Jaime and Jack Dirman. *The Jaime Escalante Math Program.* Washington, D.C.: National Education Association, 1990.

Escalante, Jaime. "Kids to be Judged by the Power of Their Dreams," *Washington Times*. 12 January 1990.

Farber, Barry A. *Crisis in Education: Stress and Burnout in the American Teacher*. San Francisco: Jossey-Bass Publishers, 1991.

Feiman-Nemser, Sharon. *Learning to Teach*. East Lansing: Michigan State University, 1983.

Finn, Chester E. *We Must Take Charge: Our Schools and Our Future*. New York: The Free Press, 1991.

Frick, Caroline. Personal Interview. 23 March 1991.

Fritz, Carleen. Personal Interview. 19 June 1991.

Gold, Mark S. *The Facts About Drugs and Alcohol*. New York: The PIA Press, 1988.

Goode, Stephan. "The Full Story of History," *Insight of the News*. 26 January 1992, pp. 12-13, 28-29.

Goodlad, John I. *Teachers for Our Nation's Schools*. San Francisco: Jossey-Bass Publishers, 1990.

Goodman, Eric. "How to Solve Our Teacher Shortage," *McCall's*. September 1990, pp. 104-110, 157-160.

Gradillas, Henry. Telephone Interview. 31 Oct. 1990.

Gruber, Craig. Personal Interview. 23 February 1991.

Headman, Jay. Personal Interview. 1 July 1991.

Henry, William A. "Upside Down in the Groves of Academe," *Time*. 1 April 1991, pp. 66-69.

Hirshberg, Charles. "Yearning to Learn," *Life*. September 1991, pp. 22-39.

Hirsch, E.D. *Cultural Literacy: What Every American Needs to Know*. Boston: Houghton Mifflin Co., 1987.

Honig, Bill. *Last Chance For Our Children: How You Can Help Save Our Schools*. Reading: Addison-Wesley Publishing Company, 1985.

Hoose, Philip. Telephone Interview. 4 April 1991

Innerst, Carol. "Two Teacher Unions Speak on Issues," *Washington Times*. 9 July 1990, p. A7.

Johnston, Dr. Lloyd D. "Summary of 1987 Drug Study Results." Media Statement, Washington, D.C., 13 January 1988.

"The Jokers Who Run Our Schools." *The Washington Monthly*. Sept. 1990, p. 12.

Jones, Diane. Personal Interview. 29 June 1991.

Jones, Fredric H. *Positive Classroom Discipline*. New York: McGraw-Hill Book Company, 1987.

Kelleher, Diane. Personal Interview. 28 July 1990.

Kimbrough, Myla. Personal Interview. 29 June 1991.

Kunjufu, Jawanza. *To be Popular and Smart: The Black Peer Group.* Chicago: African American Images, 1988.

Lambrakopoulos, Evanthia. Personal Interview. 27 June 1991.

Lapchick, Dr. Richard, Director: Northeastern University Center for the Study of Sport in Society. Telephone Interview. 2 May 1991.

Lapchick, Dr. Richard. *Pass to Play: Student Athletes and Academics.* Washington, D.C.: National Education Association, 1989.

Lewis, Anne C. "Just Rhetoric, Or a Real Issue?" *Agenda.* Winter 1992, p. 21.

Lodal, Elizabeth. Telephone Interview. 17 January 1991.

Lodal, Elizabeth. Personal Interview. 17 January 1992

Lowrie, Jeannie. Personal Interview. 29 April 1991.

Manley, Dexter. Speech, Christian Fellowship Church, Vienna, Virginia. 24 March 1991.

McCarthy, Colman. "Seeking Peaceful Solutions in the Schoolyard," *Washington Post.* 27 January 1991, p. F-4.

McFadden, Edward. "Colman McCarthy: A Passion for Peace," *The Almanac.* 7 February 1991, pp. 1, 4.

McClain, Gladys. Personal Interview. 27 June 1991.

Michael, Pamela. "From Socrates to Miss Crabtree: Teaching through the Ages," *Spectrum.* August 1990, pp. 1, 33-34.

Michener, James A. "What is the Secret of Teaching Values?" *Rediscover America.* New York: Time Magazine Co., 1991.

Nakamura, Robert. Personal Interview. 17 January 1992.

National Endowment for the Humanities. *American Memory: A Report on the Humanities in the Nation's Public Schools.* Washington, D.C.: GPO, 1987.

Novello, Antonia. "Youth and Alcohol: A National Survey." Press Conference, Washington, D.C. June 1991.

Ohanian, Susan. "Not-so-super Superintendents." *The Washington Monthly.* Sept. 1990, pp. 16-25.

Olinger, Lester. Telephone Interview. 3 March 1991.

Olson, Lynn. "Teaching Our Teachers," *Education Week.* 12 December 1990, pp. 11-26.

Owen, Nancy. 23 Sept. 1990.

Paterno, Joe. Telephone Interview. 21 April 1991.

Paterno, Sue. Telephone Interview. 17 April 1991.

Pincus, Rennie. Personal Interview. 29 April 1991.

Powell, Arthur G., Eleanor Farrar, and David K. Cohen. *The Shopping Mall High School: Winners and Losers in the Educational Marketplace.* Boston: Houghton Mifflin Company, 1985.

Powell, Nancy. Personal Interview. 19 Sept. 1990.

Rowan, Brian, "Applying Conceptions of Teaching to Organizational Reform." In *Restructuring Schools: The Next Generation of Educational Reform*. Ed. Richard F. Elmore. San Francisco: Jossey-Bass Publishers, 1990, pp. 59-96.

Schonberg, S. Kenneth. "Information About Health Factors that Affect the Way Students Learn," *NEA Today*. February 1991, p.37.

Sedlak, Michael, Christopher Wheeler, Diana Pullin, and Philip Cusick. "Bargains, Student Disengagement and Academic Learning: An Analysis of the American High School and Proposals to Raise Academic Standards." Unpublished Manuscript, Michigan State University, 1984.

Shafer, Ronald G. "An Anguished Father Recounts the Battle He Lost—Trying to Rescue a Teenage Son from Drugs," *People Weekly*. 12 March 1990.

Sheridan, Bob. Personal Interview. 92 Jan. 1992.

Shuger, Scott. "To: Sharon Pratt Dixon; From: Scott Shuger; RE: What You Need to Do Now," *The Washington Monthly*. November 1990, pp. 41-46.

Standa, Joe. Telephone Interview. 19 June 1991.

Stern, Philip M. *The Best Congress Money Can Buy*. New York: Pantheon Books, 1988.

Swinton, John. "Centre County Schools: A View from the Top," *State College Magazine*. pp. 8-14.

Sykes, Gary. "Fostering Teacher Professionalism in Schools." In *Restructuring Schools: The Next Generation of Educational Reform*. Ed. Richard F. Elmore. San Francisco: Jossey-Bass Publishers, 1990, pp. 59-96.

Tanis, Bryan. Personal Interview. 10 April 1991.

Tattel, Edie. Personal Interview. 28 May 1991.

Toffler, Alvin. *Power Shift: Knowledge, Wealth, and Violence at the Edge of the 21st Century*. New York: Bantam Books, 1990.

U.S. Department of Education. *American Education: Making it Work*. By William J. Bennett. Washington, D.C.: GPO, 1988.

U.S. Department of Education. *Choice of Schools in Six Nations: France, Netherlands, Belgium, Britain, Canada, West Germany*. Washington, D.C.: GPO, 1989.

U.S. Department of Education. The National Commission on Excellence in Education. *A Nation At Risk*. Washington, D.C.: GPO, 1983.

U.S. Department of Education. *The Nation Responds: Recent Efforts to Improve Education*. Washington, D.C.: GPO, 1984.

U.S. Department of Education. *What Works: Schools That Work: Educating Disadvantage Children*. Washington, D.C.: GPO, 1987.

U.S. Department of Education. Office of Educational Research and Improvement. *Digest of Education Statistics, 1989*. Washington, D.C.: GPO, 1989.

U.S. Department of Education. Office of Educational Research and Improvement. *Dropout Rates in the United States: 1988*. Washington, D.C.: GPO, 1989.

U.S. Department of Education. *What Works: Research About Teaching and Learning*. Washington, D.C.: GPO, 1987.

U.S. Department of Health and Human Services. Alcohol, Drug Abuse, and Mental Health Administration. *When Cocaine Affects Someone You Love*. Washington, D.C.: GPO, 1987.

Valentine, Paul W. "Hollywood's Noble Indians: Are We Dancing With Myths?" *Washington Post*. 31 March 1991, p. B-5.

Virden, Jon. Telephone Interview. 25 Sept. 1991.

Weitz, Beth. Personal Interview. 29 April 1991.

Index